Get Them to Buy:
Mastering Financial Services Marketing

AC Hoffmann

I dedicate this book to the most brilliant, funny, witty, and wacky coworkers who've made my career in financial services exciting, creative, award-winning, and memorable in ways only we can appreciate.

You know who you are.

TABLE OF CONTENTS

Introduction

In today's dynamic and highly competitive landscape, the financial services industry faces unique challenges in effectively reaching and engaging its target audience. The ability to navigate this complex environment and stand out among competitors requires a deep understanding of marketing strategies tailored specifically to the industry.

"Get Them to Buy: Mastering Financial Services Marketing" is a comprehensive guidebook designed to equip those in the financial services industry with the knowledge and tools needed to excel in their marketing efforts. Whether you are a seasoned marketing expert or a newcomer to the industry, this book will serve as your trusted resource for developing and implementing successful strategies to capture market share.

Within the pages of this book, you will discover an array of proven strategies and best practices that have helped firms thrive in a rapidly evolving marketplace. From building brand awareness and establishing a strong online presence to cultivating client relationships and measuring marketing effectiveness, each chapter delves into key aspects of financial services marketing.

The book begins by exploring the foundations of financial services marketing, highlighting the importance of adapting to the evolving marketing landscape and embracing innovative strategies to stay ahead in the industry. It then delves into market research, target audience identification, and market segmentation, providing insights on how to effectively reach and engage the right customers.

As you progress through the chapters, you will learn about the significance of crafting a compelling brand identity, creating valuable and relevant content, and leveraging digital marketing channels such as websites, social media, and email marketing. Additionally, the book addresses the ethical considerations, compliance regulations, and privacy concerns that are integral to marketing within the financial services sector.

To help you implement these strategies effectively, this book offers practical tips and actionable steps that can be customized to suit your specific organizational needs. Whether you work in banking, insurance, investment management, or any other segment of the financial services industry, the principles and insights shared in this book will empower you to elevate your marketing initiatives and achieve measurable results.

Use this book as a guide to unlock the full potential of financial services marketing. By embracing the principles outlined here, you will be well-equipped to navigate the complexities of the industry, drive customer engagement, and ultimately achieve sustainable growth and success in your marketing endeavors.

Chapter 1: The Importance of Marketing in the Financial Services Industry

Marketing plays a crucial role in the financial services industry by facilitating customer acquisition, retention, and building brand loyalty. In an increasingly competitive landscape, effective marketing strategies are essential for financial institutions, including banks, insurance companies, investment firms, and other service providers, to differentiate themselves, attract customers, and drive business growth.

Key reasons why marketing matters in financial services

Building trust and credibility
Financial services rely heavily on trust and credibility. Effective marketing enables financial institutions to establish and maintain a positive reputation in the market. Through marketing communications, transparency, and ethical practices, financial institutions can build trust among existing and potential clients, assuring them that their financial well-being is a top priority.

Customer acquisition and retention
Marketing is essential for acquiring new customers and retaining existing ones. It helps financial institutions identify their target audience, understand their needs and preferences, and develop tailored marketing campaigns to attract and engage them. By showcasing their products, services, and unique value proposition, financial institutions can differentiate themselves from competitors and convince customers to choose them over others.

Educating and informing customers
The financial services industry can be complex and intimidating for many people who do not have a background or extensive understanding of the various tools and tactics of accumulating, growing, and protecting wealth. Effective marketing efforts help simplify and demystify financial concepts by providing educational content, explaining products and services, and offering financial guidance. By empowering customers with knowledge, financial institutions can establish themselves as trusted advisors and ultimately build long-term relationships.

Creating brand awareness and recognition
Effective marketing increases brand visibility and recognition in the market. Consistent branding, messaging, and visual identity help financial institutions stand out, differentiate themselves, and stay top-of-mind among consumers. Through targeted marketing efforts, financial institutions can position themselves as industry leaders, fostering a strong brand image and attracting a loyal customer base.

Promoting innovation and adaptability
Marketing encourages financial institutions to innovate and adapt to changing market dynamics. By analyzing customer insights, market trends, and competition, financial institutions can identify emerging opportunities, develop new products or services, and enhance existing

offerings to meet evolving customer needs. Marketing research and analysis provide valuable data for informed decision-making and strategic planning.

Enhancing customer experience
Marketing plays a vital role in delivering a positive customer experience. By understanding customer expectations, financial institutions can personalize their offerings, improve service quality, and optimize customer touchpoints. Marketing-driven initiatives such as user-friendly websites, convenient mobile apps, and responsive customer support contribute to a seamless and satisfying customer journey.

Achieving business growth and objectives
Ultimately, marketing drives business growth and helps financial institutions achieve their goals and objectives. Effective marketing strategies generate leads, convert prospects into customers, increase market share, and contribute to revenue generation. By measuring marketing performance and analyzing return on investment (ROI), financial institutions can refine their strategies and optimize resource allocation for maximum impact.

Clearly, marketing plays a vital role in the financial services industry by establishing trust, acquiring and retaining customers, promoting brand awareness, fostering innovation, enhancing customer experience, and driving business growth. Embracing effective marketing strategies is essential for financial institutions to navigate the competitive landscape, adapt to changing customer needs, and build long-term success in the industry.

The evolving landscape of financial services marketing

The landscape of financial services marketing is constantly evolving due to advancements in technology, changing consumer behavior, regulatory changes, and industry trends. It's important to keep up, both with your knowledge of market trends and with your activities in the space. Here are some key factors that contribute to the evolving nature of financial services marketing:

Digital transformation
Digital transformation has had a significant impact on financial services marketing. The rise of the internet, mobile devices, and social media platforms has revolutionized how financial institutions reach and engage with their target audience. Online banking, mobile payment solutions, and digital wealth management platforms have become commonplace, requiring financial institutions to adapt their marketing strategies to cater to the digital-savvy consumer.

Data-driven marketing
With the abundance of data available, financial services marketers are increasingly relying on data analytics to drive their marketing decisions. By leveraging customer insights, market trends, and predictive analytics, financial institutions can personalize marketing messages, target specific customer segments, and deliver relevant offers and recommendations. Data-driven marketing allows for more effective and efficient campaigns, improving customer experience and increasing marketing ROI.

Personalization and customer experience
Customers today expect personalized experiences and tailored solutions. Financial services marketers are delivering personalized marketing messages, content, and offers that resonate with individual customers. And for the record, personalization goes beyond just addressing customers by name; it involves understanding their needs, preferences, and behaviors to provide relevant and timely information and recommendations. Enhancing the customer experience through seamless interactions and personalized touchpoints has become a critical competitive advantage.

Regulatory compliance
The financial services industry is subject to various regulatory requirements and compliance standards. Marketing efforts must align with regulatory guidelines, ensuring transparency, accuracy, and fair practices. Marketers need to navigate through regulations such as data protection, anti-money laundering, and privacy laws to ensure their marketing campaigns are compliant. This requires ongoing monitoring and adaptation to stay abreast of changing regulations.

Rise of FinTech and disruption
The emergence of financial technology (FinTech) companies has disrupted traditional financial services and transformed the marketing landscape. FinTech startups leverage technology, innovation, and customer-centric approaches to provide streamlined and user-friendly financial

services. Established financial institutions are embracing digital innovation and partnering with FinTech companies to enhance their marketing capabilities and offer more competitive solutions. Now more than ever the mantra "Evolve or die" has market relevance.

Social responsibility and ESG
Environmental, Social, and Governance (ESG) considerations have gained prominence in financial services marketing. Consumers are increasingly looking for financial institutions that align with their values and have a positive impact on society. Marketing efforts now emphasize social responsibility, sustainability, and ethical practices to resonate with socially conscious consumers. Navigating these waters can be tricky, since one customer's values and interests may be at odds with another's. Finding pragmatic neutrality is an art.

Shift in customer engagement channels
Traditional marketing channels such as television and print media are being complemented by digital channels and social media platforms. Financial services marketers are leveraging social media, influencer marketing, content marketing, and online communities to engage with customers, build brand loyalty, and drive conversions. Interactive chatbots and virtual assistants are also being employed to provide real-time customer support and assistance.

The evolving landscape of financial services marketing is being driven by digital transformation, data-driven marketing, personalization, regulatory compliance, FinTech disruption, ESG considerations, and changes in customer engagement channels, and it's unlikely to stop anytime soon. Successful financial services marketers must stay informed about these evolving trends, adopt innovative strategies, and embrace technology to effectively reach and engage their target audience in a data-rich, engagement-fluid market.

8 benefits of effective marketing

Effective marketing strategies play a crucial role in attracting and retaining clients for businesses in various industries, and the financial services sector is no different. There are eight key benefits of strong marketing:

1. Building brand awareness and reputation:
   Marketing efforts help create brand awareness, making potential clients aware of your financial services offerings. A strong brand presence instills confidence and trust in the minds of clients, positioning your business as a reputable and reliable provider. A positive brand reputation is instrumental in attracting new clients and retaining existing ones.

2. Targeting the right audience:
   Why spend your time and dollars barking up the wrong tree? Effective marketing allows you to identify and target your ideal client base. By conducting market research and segmentation, you can understand the specific needs, preferences, and pain points of your target audience. This knowledge enables you to tailor your marketing messages and offerings to resonate with their requirements, increasing the likelihood of attracting clients who are a good fit for your services.

3. Differentiation from competitors:
   In a competitive marketplace, effective marketing strategies help distinguish your financial services from competitors. By highlighting your unique value proposition, expertise, and distinct offerings, you can showcase why potential clients should choose your business over others. Effective marketing communicates your competitive advantages and sets you apart in a crowded market, increasing the chances of attracting clients.

4. Generating leads and conversions:
   Marketing activities such as lead generation campaigns, content marketing, search engine optimization, and advertising efforts help generate quality leads for your business. By effectively targeting and engaging your audience, you can capture the attention of potential clients and nurture them through the buyer's journey. Well-executed marketing strategies drive conversions, turning interested prospects into actual clients. Excellent, ongoing marketing keeps them loyal forever.

5. Building relationships and trust:
   Marketing plays a crucial role in building relationships with clients and fostering trust. Regular communication, informative content, and personalized interactions help establish a connection with your audience and demonstrates your interest in their success. By consistently providing value and addressing their needs, you can build long-term relationships based on trust, increasing client loyalty and the likelihood of repeat

business. This practice is the most time-consuming, but arguably the most important for helping customers understand their value to you and yours to them.

6. Enhancing customer experience:
   Effective marketing strategies prioritize delivering a positive customer experience. By understanding the needs and preferences of your clients, you can tailor your marketing efforts to provide personalized and relevant information, seamless interactions, and excellent service. A positive customer experience leads to client satisfaction, advocacy, and increased client retention. (We all know what a negative customer experience leads to, and social media makes it all too easy for them to share about it.)

7. Upselling and cross-selling opportunities:
   Marketing strategies can also drive upselling and cross-selling opportunities with existing clients. By maintaining ongoing communication and demonstrating the value of additional services or products, you can expand the scope of your relationship with clients. Effective marketing keeps clients informed about new offerings, upgrades, or complementary services, encouraging them to explore additional options with your business. Do right by customers and they will be more likely to give you more and bigger ways to serve them.

8. Adaptation to market changes:
   The financial services landscape is dynamic, with evolving client needs and industry trends. Effective marketing strategies enable businesses to stay agile and adapt to changing market conditions. By continuously monitoring the market, gathering client feedback, and analyzing data, you can refine your marketing strategies and offerings to remain relevant and meet client expectations.

Use marketing to its full potential to attract and retain clients and achieve all eight of these business-critical benefits. By investing in strategic and well-executed marketing efforts, financial services businesses can grow and thrive alongside their customers.

Chapter 2: Understanding the Financial Services Landscape

The financial services industry encompasses a wide range of sectors, each offering unique products, services, and opportunities. Understanding and exploring these sectors can provide valuable insights into the diverse landscape of the industry. Let's discern and differentiate the key sectors within the industry.

Banking
Banking is one of the fundamental sectors within the financial services industry. It includes commercial banks, retail banks, investment banks, and credit unions. Banking services cover a broad spectrum, such as savings accounts, checking accounts, loans, mortgages, credit cards, investment products, and wealth management services. Exploring the banking sector allows individuals to understand the core functions of deposit-taking, lending, and financial intermediation.

Insurance
The insurance sector focuses on risk management and protection against potential financial losses. It includes life insurance, health insurance, property and casualty insurance, auto insurance, and more. Insurance companies provide policies that offer coverage and financial compensation in the event of specified risks or events. Exploring the insurance sector helps individuals understand the principles of risk assessment, underwriting, policy management, and claims settlement.

Investment and asset management
The investment and asset management sector involves managing and growing clients' investments and portfolios. This sector includes asset management firms, mutual funds, hedge funds, pension funds, and private equity firms. Professionals in this sector make investment decisions, conduct research, perform portfolio analysis, and provide investment advisory services. Exploring this sector introduces individuals to investment strategies, financial markets, asset classes, and the importance of risk management.

Financial planning and advisory
The financial planning and advisory sector focuses on helping individuals and businesses achieve their financial goals. Financial planners, wealth advisors, and financial advisors provide guidance on budgeting, retirement planning, tax planning, estate planning, and investment strategies. Exploring this sector offers insights into personal finance, financial goal setting, asset allocation, and the importance of comprehensive financial planning.

Payment systems and technology
The payment systems and technology sector encompasses electronic payment solutions, mobile banking, digital wallets, payment processors, and fintech companies. This sector has revolutionized the way financial transactions are conducted, providing convenience, security, and efficiency. Exploring this sector exposes individuals to innovations in payment methods, blockchain technology, cybersecurity, and the evolving landscape of digital financial services.

Real estate and mortgage
The real estate and mortgage sector involves the financing, buying, selling, and development of properties. It includes mortgage lenders, real estate brokers, property management firms, and real estate investment trusts (REITs). Understanding this sector introduces individuals to mortgage lending processes, property valuation, real estate investment strategies, and the dynamics of the housing market.

Financial technology (FinTech)
The FinTech sector combines technology and financial services to deliver innovative solutions. It includes online lending platforms, robo-advisors, digital banks, crowdfunding platforms, and blockchain-based financial systems. Exploring this sector offers insights into the disruptive potential of technology in areas such as lending, payments, wealth management, and financial inclusion.

Regulatory and compliance
The regulatory and compliance sector crisscrosses all the others as it focuses on ensuring adherence to laws, regulations, and industry standards within the financial services industry. It includes regulatory bodies, compliance departments within financial institutions, and consulting firms specializing in regulatory matters. Understanding this sector helps individuals grasp the importance of regulatory frameworks, risk management, compliance procedures, and ethical practices.

Exploring the different sectors of the financial services industry provides a comprehensive understanding of the industry's breadth and depth. It offers insights into the various career opportunities available, the interconnectedness of sectors, and the evolving landscape as it is shaped by technological advancements, regulatory changes, and customer needs. By gaining knowledge about these sectors, marketers and individuals alike can make informed decisions about their career paths, financial choices, and engagement with a diversity of financial services companies.

Chapter 3: Identifying Your Target Audience and Market Segmentation

In financial services marketing, understanding the target audience and implementing effective market segmentation strategies are essential for reaching and engaging the right customers. By identifying the target audience and segmenting the market, financial service providers can tailor their marketing efforts to meet the specific needs, preferences, and behaviors of different customer groups. Here's an overview of the process:

Identify the target audience

Start by examining the demographic characteristics of the target audience, such as age, gender, income, education level, occupation, and location. This information helps in understanding the basic profile of the target customers.

- Psychographics: Dive deeper into the psychographic aspects of the target audience, including their values, attitudes, lifestyle choices, and behaviors. Understand their motivations, aspirations, financial goals, and pain points.
- Customer Data and Insights: Utilize customer data from internal sources, such as transaction history, customer surveys, and feedback, to gain insights into the preferences, behaviors, and needs of existing customers. This data can help identify common traits and patterns among your target audience.

Market segmentation
To further drill down into key audiences and strengthen homogeneity therein, group them according to:

- Geographic Segmentation: Divide the market into geographic segments based on location, such as countries, regions, cities, or even as granularly as specific neighborhoods. Consider geographical factors that may influence financial needs and preferences, such as economic conditions, cultural differences, and regulatory variations.
- Demographic Segmentation: Further segment the target audience based on demographic factors such as age, gender, income, occupation, education level, and family size. This segmentation allows for more targeted marketing messages and customized offerings based on specific demographic characteristics.
- Psychographic Segmentation: Segment the market based on psychographic variables such as values, attitudes, interests, lifestyles, and behavioral patterns. Understand the unique motivations, goals, and challenges of different customer segments to tailor marketing messages that resonate with their specific needs and preferences.
- Behavioral Segmentation: Analyze customer behavior to segment the market based on patterns of purchasing, product usage, engagement with financial services, and response to marketing campaigns. This segmentation can help identify customer segments with similar behaviors and preferences, allowing for more personalized marketing approaches.

Targeting and positioning

Target Market Selection
Figure out where to focus your efforts. Based on the identified segments, evaluate the potential value and attractiveness of each segment. Consider factors such as size, growth potential, profitability, competition, and alignment with the organization's capabilities and objectives. You may choose more than one at a time, but avoid spreading your efforts and budget too thin.

Positioning strategy
Develop a positioning strategy for each target segment. Positioning involves crafting a unique value proposition and differentiating your offer from competitors within each segment. Highlight the specific benefits, solutions, or advantages that resonate with the needs and preferences of the target audience.

Customizing marketing efforts
Marketing is most effective when it feels less "marketing-ish" and more like a personal conversation. To help with that, try to customize your messages as much as possible without being completely inefficient with far too many iterations.

Messaging and communication
Craft marketing messages and content that speak directly to the identified target audience and their specific needs. Tailor the language, tone, and style of communication to resonate with the targeted segments. You will and should speak to a 22-year-old career-builder differently than a 72-year-old retiree.

Product and service offerings
Customize your financial products, services, and solutions to meet the unique requirements of each segment. Consider features, pricing, bundling options, and delivery channels that align with the preferences and expectations of the target audience. One size never fits all.

Channel selection
Determine the most effective marketing channels to reach the target segments. This may include digital channels (websites, social media, email marketing), traditional media (TV, radio, print), direct marketing, events, or partnerships with relevant organizations.

Continuously monitor and assess the effectiveness of the target audience identification and market segmentation strategies. Adjust and refine your approaches based on customer feedback, market changes, and evolving customer needs to ensure ongoing relevance and success. If it's not working, don't be afraid to change course. As Ross would say, "Pivot!"

Market trends, consumer behaviors, and regulatory considerations

In the financial services industry, staying informed about market trends, understanding consumer behaviors, and keeping up with regulatory considerations are crucial for sound decision-making and intelligent marketing. The heads of your organization's marketing function should lead the charge by using trade organizations, industry or proprietary research, and professional connections to conduct ongoing analysis in these three key areas:

1. Market trends analysis
    - **Economic factors:** Monitor macroeconomic indicators, such as interest rates, inflation rates, GDP growth, and employment data, to understand the overall economic environment and its potential impact on consumer behavior and financial needs.

    - **Technological advancements:** Stay updated on emerging technologies and digital innovations that are reshaping the financial services landscape. Analyze trends in mobile banking, fintech solutions, artificial intelligence, blockchain, and data analytics to identify opportunities for improving customer experiences and streamlining processes.

    - **Changing customer preferences:** Study shifts in consumer preferences, expectations, and demands within the financial industry. Analyze trends related to personalization, convenience, sustainability, social responsibility, and digital experiences to align marketing strategies with evolving customer needs.

2. Consumer behaviors analysis:
    - **Customer Segmentation:** Utilize market research, customer surveys, and data analytics to segment customers based on their behaviors, preferences, needs, and financial goals. Identify patterns and trends within each segment to tailor marketing efforts and develop targeted campaigns.

    - **Customer Journey Mapping:** Understand the customer journey and touchpoints to identify pain points, opportunities for improvement, and moments where marketing interventions can positively influence customer decisions. Analyze consumer behaviors throughout the decision-making process, from awareness and consideration to conversion and retention.

    - **Data Analytics:** Leverage data analytics tools and techniques to gain insights into customer behaviors, purchase patterns, cross-selling opportunities, and customer lifetime value. Utilize predictive analytics to anticipate customer needs, personalize marketing messages, and enhance customer experiences.

3. Regulatory considerations:
    - **Compliance and legal frameworks:** Stay informed about regulatory requirements, laws, and industry standards that govern the financial services sector. Understand the

implications of regulations such as consumer protection laws, data privacy regulations, anti-money laundering (AML) regulations, and know-your-customer (KYC) requirements. Ensure marketing practices align with legal and ethical standards.

- **Consumer trust and security:** Analyze consumer sentiments and concerns related to data privacy, security, and trust. Stay proactive in addressing these concerns through transparent communication, secure technology infrastructure, and compliance with data protection regulations.
- **Industry Changes and Updates:** Monitor regulatory changes and updates within the financial services industry. Understand the impact of new regulations on marketing practices, customer communications, product offerings, and compliance requirements. Stay engaged with industry associations, regulatory bodies, and professional networks to stay informed about the evolving regulatory landscape.

By analyzing market trends, consumer behaviors, and regulatory considerations, financial services marketers can make informed decisions, develop effective marketing strategies, and build strong relationships with their target audience. This analysis helps in identifying market opportunities, addressing customer needs, mitigating risks, and ensuring compliance with relevant regulations. It also enables organizations to stay ahead of the competition, enhance customer experiences, and build trust and credibility in a saturated market.

Chapter 4: Developing a Comprehensive Marketing Strategy

A comprehensive marketing strategy is a strategic approach that encompasses all aspects of marketing to achieve organizational goals and objectives. It involves careful planning, analysis, and implementation of various marketing tactics to effectively reach and engage the target audience.

Think of it as a roadmap that guides organizations in achieving their marketing objectives. It starts with a thorough understanding of the target audience, market dynamics, and competitive landscape. By conducting market research and analysis, businesses can identify opportunities, assess customer needs, and determine the most effective marketing approaches.

In developing their strategy, organizations define a unique value proposition and brand position. This includes identifying the key messages, benefits, and competitive advantages they want to communicate to their target audience. A strong brand identity and correct positioning help differentiate the business from competitors and create a consistent and compelling image in the market.

A brand's strategy should encompass various marketing channels and tactics, including a mix of traditional and digital marketing approaches such as advertising, public relations, social media marketing, content marketing, email marketing, search engine optimization, and more. The selection of channels and tactics depends on the target audience, industry trends, and budget.

It should also include setting clear and *measurable* goals, because otherwise, how do you know if you've been doing things well or less well? These goals can be related to increasing brand awareness, generating leads, driving sales, improving customer retention, or enhancing customer satisfaction. By setting specific and measurable goals, organizations can evaluate the effectiveness of their marketing efforts and make informed decisions for future campaigns.

Regular monitoring, analysis, and optimization are essential components of a proper marketing strategy. Organizations need to track and analyze key performance indicators (KPIs) to assess the success of their marketing activities and make data-driven adjustments. This iterative process ensures that the marketing strategy remains aligned with the changing market landscape and customer preferences.

Simply put, don't skip the strategy: It is a vital framework that enables organizations to effectively plan, implement, and evaluate marketing efforts. It considers the target audience, market dynamics, competitive landscape, and goals of the business. By developing a strategic and cohesive approach, organizations can maximize their impact, build brand awareness, generate leads, and *ding-ding-ding!* drive business growth. After all, isn't that the point?

Setting a clear target

Identifying clear goals and objectives is essential for guiding and measuring the success of a marketing strategy. It's worth the time and effort to deliberately ponder goals that will be meaningful to your firm. Not all goals are worthy.

Here's a step-by-step process to help you set clear and effective goals:

1. Understand the Business Objectives:
Start by understanding the broader business objectives that the marketing goals should align with. These could be increasing revenue, expanding market share, launching a new product, improving customer satisfaction, or enhancing brand reputation. Keep this objective front and center as you progress through the goal-setting process.

2. Make Goals Specific and Measurable:
Ensure that each marketing goal is specific and clearly defined. Vague goals make it difficult to track progress and evaluate success. For example, instead of stating "Increase brand awareness," specify "Increase brand awareness by 20% among the target audience within six months."

Make goals measurable by attaching quantifiable metrics or key performance indicators (KPIs) to them. This allows for objective evaluation and comparison of results. For instance, "Generate 500 new leads per month" or "Achieve a 15% increase in website traffic within three months."

3. Ensure Goals are Realistic and Attainable:
Set goals that are realistic and attainable based on the available resources, budget, and market conditions. Unrealistic goals can demotivate the team and hinder progress. Consider factors such as market competition, industry benchmarks, and historical performance when setting goals. You may even consider "bucketing" goals into immediate, near-term, and long-term goals, and then revisit as resources become available. It's better for morale to achieve smaller goals regularly than keep missing the mark on big ones.

4. Establish a Timeframe:
Assign a specific timeframe or deadline to each goal. This provides a sense of urgency and helps prioritize efforts. For example, "Increase social media engagement by 30% within three months" or "Achieve a 10% increase in customer retention by the end of the fiscal year."

5. Align Goals with Target Audience and Marketing Strategy:
Ensure that the goals are aligned with the target audience and the overall marketing strategy. Consider the needs, preferences, and behaviors of the target audience when defining the goals. Aligning goals with the marketing strategy ensures consistency and coherence across all marketing activities.

6. Break Down Goals into Actionable Objectives:
Break down each goal into smaller, actionable objectives or milestones. This makes the goals more manageable and enables progress tracking. Assign responsibilities and timelines for achieving each objective. This practice falls into the Lao Tzu philosophy of "the journey of a thousand miles begins with a single step".

7. Regularly Monitor and Evaluate Progress:
Continuously monitor and evaluate progress towards the goals. Use analytics, tracking tools, and performance indicators to measure and assess the success of marketing efforts. Adjust strategies and tactics as needed based on the insights gained from monitoring.

Remember that setting goals is an iterative process, meaning it's not a set-it-and-forget-it exercise. Regularly review and reassess the goals to ensure they remain relevant, realistic, and aligned with the changing business landscape. By setting clear and measurable goals, organizations can focus their efforts, motivate their teams, and effectively evaluate the impact of their marketing initiatives.

Conducting market research and competitive analysis
Market research and competitive analysis are vital components of developing an effective marketing strategy. They provide valuable insights into the target market, consumer behavior, industry trends, and competitors.

The process of conducting market research and competitive analysis can take time, and is necessarily on-going since markets never stagnate. To begin conducting your analysis, follow these eight steps:

1. Define Research Objectives:
Clearly define the objectives of your market research and competitive analysis. Determine what specific information you need to gather and the purpose behind it. This could include understanding customer preferences, identifying market opportunities, evaluating product demand, or assessing the competitive landscape.

2. Identify Data Sources:
Identify relevant data sources for your research. This may include primary research (surveys, interviews, focus groups) or secondary research (industry reports, market studies, government data, academic publications). Consider utilizing a combination of qualitative and quantitative research methods for a comprehensive understanding, and be sure you tap reputable resources whose findings you can trust.

3. Understand the Target Market:
Start by defining your target market and understanding its characteristics, demographics, psychographics, and behaviors. Gather data on consumer preferences, needs, pain points, and

buying patterns. Surveys, interviews, and actual customer feedback can be the best ways to
gain insights directly from your target audience. In other words, ask them!

4. Analyze Industry Trends:

Stay informed about the latest trends and developments in the industry. Monitor market
reports, industry publications, news articles, and online resources to identify emerging trends,
shifts in consumer behavior, technological advancements, regulatory changes, and other
relevant factors that may impact your marketing strategy. (Your synthesis of this information,
filtered through the lens of your subject matter expertise, can make for wonderful thought-
leadership opportunities with articles, interviews or white papers.)

5. Evaluate Competitors:

Conduct a competitive analysis to understand the strengths, weaknesses, strategies, and
offerings of your competitors. Identify direct competitors as well as potential disruptors in the
market. Analyze their positioning, pricing, marketing tactics, distribution channels, and
customer experiences. This information can help identify gaps in the market and differentiate
your offerings. Keeping a finger on the pulse of what's happening around you can help prevent
your firm and business model from being blindsided.

6. Gather and Analyze Data:

Collect the relevant data from your chosen sources. Organize and analyze the data to identify
key patterns, trends, and insights. Utilize tools such as data visualization, statistical analysis, and
market research software to interpret and extract meaningful information from the data.
Artificial intelligence models may help make this process faster, but never discount the
extrapolation and seemingly incongruous connections an experienced human analysis can
uncover.

7. Make Informed Decisions:

Based on the insights gained from your market research and competitive analysis, your team
will be able to draw conclusions and make informed decisions about your marketing strategy.
Identify market opportunities, potentially different target segments, areas for differentiation,
and strategies to gain a competitive advantage.

8. Monitor and Update:

Market research and competitive analysis are ongoing processes. Continuously monitor
changes in the market, consumer preferences, and competitive landscape. Regularly update
your research and analysis to stay ahead of industry trends, customer needs, and competitors'
strategies. The work is never done.

A disciplined practice of ongoing research and analysis, can help firms gain a deep
understanding of their ideal audience, identify opportunities, make informed decisions, and
develop effective strategies to reach them. Without this knowledge and confidence, your

organization will struggle to create meaningful messages, deliver superior customer experiences, or stay truly competitive in the dynamic marketplace.

Where to find research help and who to hire
If, like many others, your firm does not have the skills or resources in-house to conduct market research and competitive analysis, there are several options for hiring professionals or agencies specializing in these areas. Here are a few options to consider:

Market Research Firms
Market research firms specialize in conducting research studies, collecting data, and providing insights and analysis. They have expertise in various research methodologies and can tailor their approach to meet your specific needs. Research firms can handle both qualitative and quantitative research, including surveys, focus groups, and data analysis.

Consulting Firms
Management consulting firms often have dedicated teams that offer market research and competitive analysis services. These firms can provide strategic guidance, research capabilities, and industry expertise to help you understand your target market, competitors, and industry trends. They can also assist in translating the research findings into actionable recommendations, which is key.

Freelance Market Researchers
Freelance market researchers are independent professionals who offer their services on a project basis. They bring expertise in research methodologies, data collection, and analysis. Platforms like Upwork, Freelancer, or LinkedIn can help you find and connect with qualified freelancers who specialize in market research and competitive analysis.

Academic Institutions
Consider reaching out to universities or colleges with marketing or business departments. Many academic institutions have faculty members and students who can conduct market research as part of their academic projects or research initiatives. Collaborating with academic institutions can provide access to resources and fresh perspectives.

Industry Associations
Industry associations or trade organizations related to your specific industry may offer market research services or have partnerships with research firms. They can provide valuable insights and reports based on their expertise and industry connections.

Boutique Marketing Agencies
If you have relationships with boutique marketing agencies, they may offer market research and competitive analysis services as part of their suite. Consult with them to see if they have the expertise and resources to conduct the research you require.

When selecting a provider for market research and competitive analysis, consider their experience, track record, industry knowledge, and the specific services they offer. Biggest is not always best if you require personalized attention and collaboration. Request proposals and/or conduct interviews to ensure they understand your objectives and can deliver the insights and analysis you need. Ultimately, choose a provider who aligns with your goals, budget, and timeline, and who can deliver actionable recommendations to support your marketing strategy.

Chapter 5: Defining your UVP and positioning statement

Defining a unique value proposition (UVP) and positioning statement is crucial for effectively communicating your brand's value and differentiation to your target audience. You may find that you do not stand out in obvious ways, but it's likely that you either operate a bit differently or provide a unique offer for clients. Begin defining (and honing) your edge with these eight steps.

1.   Match Your Target Audience

There is no point in promoting your firm to unlikely clients. Accept that you will not be the right fit for every audience, then sift until you find your most fruitful prospects. This exercise is less about trying to become "right" for an audience and more about finding the audience for whom you are already right. Examine the needs, preferences, pain points, aspirations and resistance of the audience you have targeted and then decide if your offer fits the bill. Does it solve their problem, make life easier, match their level of sophistication, and resonate with their primary needs? If the answers are yes, continue. If the answers are no, find an alternative audience.

2.   Identify Your Competitive Advantage:

Brazenly evaluate your products, services, and brand to identify what sets you apart from your competitors. Bear in mind that you may not be completely objective about your organization, and you may want to bring in outsiders to provide agnostic feedback. It's important to determine your unique strengths, whether it's superior quality, innovative features, exceptional customer service, competitive pricing, or any other aspect that provides value to your target audience. You may inadvertently discover blind spots or weaknesses as you work to identify strengths—think of these as opportunities for growth and improvement.

3.   Define Your UVP:

After identifying your competitive advantage, it is time to develop your unique value proposition—a concise statement that communicates the specific value your brand delivers to customers. It should highlight the unique benefits or solutions your offering provides, addressing your target audience's needs in a way that separates you from competitors. Keep it clear, compelling, and customer-centric. (Later, we'll discuss the risk of not creating a UVP)

Focus on key benefits or outcomes your target audience can expect by choosing your brand. Consider both functional and emotional benefits and how they align with your audience's desires and aspirations. Focus on what makes your brand special and valuable to your customers.

4.   Craft Your Positioning Statement:

The positioning statement is a brief, clear, and memorable statement that summarizes your brand's unique position in the market and how it fulfills customer needs. It should capture the essence of your UVP and differentiate your brand from competitors. Include the target audience, their specific needs, the unique value your brand offers, and the reason why customers should choose you. Ironically, this statement is intended to be broad and specific simultaneously.

5. Test and Refine:

Once you have drafted your UVP and positioning statement, test them with your target audience. Gather feedback, conduct surveys or focus groups to see if that UVP has clicked. Maybe it will, maybe it won't. Rather than marrying yourself to your own ideas, it's so important to stay nimble and be ready to refine and iterate based on feedback to ensure clarity, relevance, and effectiveness.

6. Consistency and Integration

Ensure that your UVP and positioning statement are consistently integrated across all your marketing communications and touchpoints. Use them in your website, social media, advertising campaigns, and other marketing materials to create a unified and compelling brand message. Continuously ask yourself if the materials you put out support your UVP and position. Be prepared to stick with your direction for at least a year. Not only will it need time to gain traction and recognition, but changing course often can completely confuse your audience and make your brand look amateurish.

7. Regularly Review and Adapt:

Market dynamics and customer preferences evolve over time, so regularly review and adapt your UVP and positioning statement to stay relevant and competitive. Monitor changes in the market, customer feedback, and competitor strategies to identify opportunities for refinement and improvement. Note the choice of words: refinement and improvement. Your UVP and positioning statement may need a bit of a tweak, but don't throw the baby out with the bathwater. If you've properly gone through the exercise of creating them, you shouldn't need to make a wholesale change. You may just need some minor finesse. Proceed with caution.

Remember, your UVP and positioning statement should be always, always, always be customer-focused, clear, and distinct. They should resonate with your target audience and create a strong perception of value and differentiation. By defining a compelling UVP and positioning statement, you can effectively communicate your brand's unique offering and establish a strong market position.

The risks of not setting yourself apart

A brand that fails to establish a unique value proposition faces several risks and challenges in the market, such as:

Lack of Differentiation: Without a clear UVP, a brand may struggle to differentiate itself from competitors. It becomes difficult for customers to distinguish the brand from others offering similar products or services. As a result, the brand gets lost in the crowded marketplace and fails to stand out. Being chosen by customers will me more about luck than skill.

Increased Price Sensitivity: Without a unique value proposition, the brand becomes vulnerable to price-based competition. Customers may perceive the brand's offerings as interchangeable with those of competitors, leading them to make purchase decisions primarily based on price. This can erode profit margins and make it challenging to maintain sustainable growth.

Weak Brand Identity: A strong UVP contributes to a brand's identity and positioning. It helps customers understand what the brand represents, the value it delivers, and why they should choose it over alternatives. Without a compelling UVP, the brand's identity may be unclear or weak, leading to a lack of customer engagement and brand loyalty.

Ineffective Marketing Messaging: A well-defined UVP serves as the foundation for marketing messaging. It allows brands to craft compelling and targeted communications that resonate with their target audience. Without a clear UVP, marketing messages can become generic, confusing, or irrelevant, resulting in ineffective campaigns and difficulty in attracting and retaining customers.

Missed Opportunities: Brands without a UVP may miss out on opportunities to capitalize on specific market segments or customer needs. A UVP helps identify and target niche markets or underserved customer segments, enabling brands to tailor their offerings and marketing strategies accordingly. Without a clear UVP, brands may fail to leverage these opportunities and lose potential customers to competitors.

Lack of Customer Loyalty: A strong UVP helps build customer loyalty by creating a unique and valuable experience. Without a compelling UVP, customers may not develop a strong affinity for the brand and may be more likely to switch to competitors that offer a clearer value proposition. This can lead to reduced customer retention and a constant need to attract new customers.

To mitigate these risks, it is essential for brands to invest time and effort into establishing a unique value proposition that sets them apart from competitors and resonates with their target audience. A well-defined UVP makes brands easily recognizable and helps create customer loyalty as well as drive long-term success in the market.

Crafting a compelling brand identity for the financial services firm

Now that you know all the reasons to spend time and effort creating a compelling brand identity (and the risks of not doing so), how do you proceed? Prepare to be thoughtful and strategic, but also methodical. Begin here:

1. Define Your Brand Values and Personality:
Start by defining the core values and personality traits that you want your financial services firm to embody. Consider the qualities you want to be known for, such as trustworthiness, expertise, innovation, or client-centricity. These values will form the foundation of your brand identity. Are you a thought leader? Are you committed to simplifying complex ideas? Is your brand the easiest and most convenient to work with? Prioritize your values and what you can realistically (and consistently) deliver.

2. Understand Your Target Audience:
Gain a deep understanding of your target audience—their demographics, psychographics, needs, and preferences. Determine how your brand can fulfill their specific needs and aspirations. This understanding will help you tailor your brand identity to resonate with your audience. If your brands value convenience above all else and you're unable to deliver that, either you must modify your operation or your target audience.

3. Develop a Compelling Brand Story:
Craft a compelling narrative that communicates your brand's purpose, history, and unique value proposition. Your brand story should connect with your target audience on an emotional level and showcase how your financial services firm can make a difference in their lives or businesses. For example, there are financial services firms who focus on serving military families, teachers or non-profit workers. That's a story worth telling. What's yours?

4. Create a Distinctive Visual Identity:
Design a visually appealing and distinctive brand identity that represents or reinvigorates your financial services firm. This includes creating a logo, selecting colors, typography, and visual elements that convey the desired message and evoke the desired emotions. Ensure that your visual identity is consistent across all brand touchpoints. No matter where they are in their journey, it should be clear who customers are interacting with.

5. Establish Brand Messaging:
Develop clear and consistent messaging that communicates your brand's value and resonates with your target audience. Craft compelling taglines, key messages, and value propositions that differentiate your financial services firm from competitors. Use language that is easily understood and aligns with your brand personality. The tone you choose should be communicated internally in a style guide so everyone tasked with communicating on behalf of your brand can do so seamlessly.

6.   Deliver Consistent Brand Experience:

Consistency is key in building a strong brand identity. Ensure that all interactions and touchpoints with your audience reflect your brand values and personality. This includes your website, social media presence, marketing materials, customer service, and any other customer-facing channels. Consistency builds trust and reinforces your brand identity. Employees and contractors should have clear guidelines to keep the brand tight.

7.   Build Thought Leadership and Expertise:

If possible, establish your financial services firm as a thought leader and expert in your field. Share valuable insights, industry knowledge, and educational content through blogs, articles, whitepapers, webinars, or speaking engagements. Positioning your brand as a trusted authority enhances its credibility and attracts clients, and most importantly, it gives you many reasons and opportunities to stay in front of prospects without spamming them with mindless drivel.

8.   Foster Strong Relationships:

This should be common sense, but so often it's overlooked. As a professional services organization, you absolutely should work to build strong and lasting relationships with your clients. Provide excellent service, personalized solutions, and consistent communication. Actively listen to your clients' needs and feedback, and continuously strive to exceed their expectations. Empower employees to provide excellent, solution-driven service, and you'll be remembered. Positive client experiences and word-of-mouth referrals absolutely enhance your brand identity.

9.   Monitor and Adapt:

Continuously monitor market trends, customer feedback, and industry developments. Stay agile and tweak your brand identity as needed to remain relevant and competitive. Regularly evaluate the effectiveness of your brand identity efforts and make necessary adjustments. These adjustments may not be so much about changing your brand as changing the way you present your brand in the market.

Crafting a compelling brand identity for your financial services firm requires a deep understanding of your target audience, a clear articulation of your unique value proposition, and consistent delivery of a brand experience that aligns with your values and personality. By developing a strong identity, you can differentiate yourself in the market and foster trust and loyalty among your clients.

Chapter 6: Building a Strong Online Presence

In the ever-evolving digital landscape, building a strong online presence has become a vital imperative for financial services firms. The internet has transformed the way people seek and interact with financial information, products, and services. As a result, establishing a robust and compelling online presence is no longer a luxury but a necessity for success.

The importance of a strong online presence for financial services firms cannot be overstated. It serves as a powerful tool to attract and engage with potential clients, build trust, and differentiate your brand in a competitive marketplace. With the majority of consumers conducting online research before making financial decisions, a well-crafted online presence can significantly impact your visibility, credibility, and ultimately, your bottom line.

Your online presence offers an opportunity to showcase your firm's expertise, offerings, and value proposition to a vast audience. Through informative and engaging content, a carefully designed website, and active participation in relevant digital channels, companies can establish themselves as trusted authorities and thought leaders in their respective niches. By sharing valuable insights, educational resources, and timely market updates, your organization can become a reliable and sought-after source—one that is transparent, trusted, and respected.

Moreover, a strong online presence enables financial services firms to adapt to changing consumer behaviors and preferences. With the rise of digital technologies and the increasing reliance on mobile devices, clients now expect convenient and accessible solutions. By offering user-friendly online platforms, mobile applications, and digital tools, firms can cater to the evolving needs of their clients and deliver personalized experiences.

More than ever, a strong online presence allows financial services firms to leverage digital marketing strategies to reach a wider audience. Through search engine optimization (SEO), targeted advertising, and social media engagement, firms can expand their reach, connect with potential clients, and generate leads. By nurturing these relationships through effective online communication, firms can convert prospects into loyal clients and advocates.

Lastly, let's not forget that an online presence makes it easy for financial services firms to collect valuable data and insights. Through website analytics, social media metrics, and customer feedback, firms can gain a deeper understanding of their audience, identify trends, and refine their marketing and service strategies. These data-driven insights enable firms to make informed decisions, optimize their offerings, and continuously enhance the client experience.

It's important to take your online presence seriously, and worthwhile to invest in its consistency and success. Doing so will make it possible to attract and engage with clients, but also positions firms as industry leaders, facilitates strategic pivots to better serve changing consumer preferences, and drives business growth. By embracing the power of the digital realm, financial services firms can thrive in a highly competitive landscape while building lasting relationships with their clients.

Leveraging digital marketing channels: websites, social media, and email marketing

Financial services firms can leverage various digital marketing channels, including websites, social media, and email marketing, to effectively reach and engage their target audience. Here are some ways to harness the power of these channels:

Websites:
- Create or update a professional and user-friendly website that serves as a central hub for your brand and offerings.
- Optimize your website for search engines (SEO) to improve visibility and organic (un-paid-for) traffic.
- Provide valuable and informative content, such as blog articles, whitepapers, or educational resources, to establish your expertise and attract visitors.
- Showcase your services, testimonials, case studies, and success stories to build credibility and trust.
- Incorporate clear calls-to-action (CTAs) to encourage visitors to take desired actions, such as contacting you or subscribing to your newsletter.
- Implement lead generation forms to capture visitor information and nurture leads with a sales funnel.

*Don't let your site go stale. Think of it as a living breathing 24/7 marketing tool that can help you prospect even while your team sleeps.

Social Media:
- Identify the social media platforms that align with your target audience's preferences and demographics. It is more important to use one or two well than to try to be everywhere all the time (unless, of course, you have an inexhaustible budget for a team of 24/7/365 social media mavens).
- Establish a consistent presence on these platforms and regularly post engaging content, such as industry insights, tips, news, or thought leadership pieces.
- Interact with your audience by responding to comments, messages, and inquiries in a timely manner. This will make it seem like there are real live people behind your brand. Better yet, in this day and age of AI, try to put some actual real live people behind your brand because bots tend to annoy customers.
- Deploy social media advertising to reach a wider audience, target specific demographics, and promote your services or content.
- Join relevant industry groups or communities to network, share knowledge, and establish yourself as an expert. Be helpful and positive without expectation.

- Leverage social media analytics to track engagement, measure the effectiveness of your campaigns, and refine your strategies.

Email Marketing:
- Build a quality email subscriber list by offering valuable incentives, such as exclusive content, downloadable resources, or special promotions. Everyone likes to feel special.
- Segment your email list based on demographics, interests, or client preferences to deliver targeted and personalized messages.
- Develop a consistent email marketing strategy that includes regular newsletters, updates on industry trends, educational content, or personalized offers. But don't "spam" people with excessive content that makes you seem overbearing.
- Craft compelling subject lines and engaging email content to encourage open rates and click-throughs. A/B test lines to see which ones garner more responses.
- Implement marketing automation to streamline your email campaigns, such as sending personalized messages triggered by specific actions or milestones.
- Monitor email performance metrics, including open rates, click-through rates, and conversions, to evaluate the effectiveness of your campaigns and make data-driven improvements.

By leveraging digital channels, financial services marketers can effectively reach their key audience, establish thought leadership, build credibility, and generate leads. It's important to maintain a consistent brand voice, provide valuable content, and engage with your audience to foster strong relationships and drive business growth. Regularly analyze and optimize your digital marketing efforts to ensure maximum impact and return on investment—and be sure to ask customers what they actually want or don't want. Listen to them.

Creating engaging and informative content for online platforms

Creating engaging and informative content for online platforms is crucial for capturing and retaining the attention of your audience.

10 Tips to Make your Content Compelling

1. Know who you're talking to: Understand your target audience's demographics, interests, pain points, and preferences. This knowledge will guide your content creation process and ensure it resonates with your intended prospects.

2. Provide value: Focus on delivering valuable and relevant content that solves problems, answers questions, or provides insights. Offer practical tips, industry trends, how-to guides, or thought-provoking perspectives that your audience can benefit from.

3. Use storytelling techniques: Humans are wired to connect with stories. Incorporate storytelling techniques to make your content more engaging and memorable. Use anecdotes, real-life examples, or case studies to illustrate your points and evoke emotions.

4. Make it visually appealing: Visual elements can enhance the appeal of your content. Use high-quality images, infographics, videos, or charts to present information in an attractive and easily digestible format.

5. Keep it concise and scannable: Online readers have limited attention spans. Make your content easy to consume by using clear headings, subheadings, bullet points, and short paragraphs. Break up text with visual elements to make it more scannable.

6. Use an authentic and conversational tone: Write in a conversational tone to make your content more relatable and approachable. Avoid using jargon or complex language that may alienate or confuse your audience. It doesn't make you seem smarter.

7. Incorporate multimedia elements: Don't limit your content to text alone. Utilize multimedia elements like videos, podcasts, or interactive tools to provide a dynamic and engaging experience for your audience. Everyone learns differently.

8. Include calls-to-action (CTAs): Guide your audience on the next steps by including clear and compelling CTAs. Encourage them to share your content, subscribe to your newsletter, sign up for a webinar, or contact you for more information.

9. Encourage audience interaction: Foster engagement by inviting your audience to comment, ask questions, or share their experiences related to the content. Respond to comments and encourage conversations to create a sense of community.

10. Measure and analyze: Use analytics tools to measure the performance of your content. Track metrics like page views, time on page, social shares, and engagement to understand what resonates with your audience. Use this data to refine and improve your content strategy.

The key to creating engaging and informative content is to put your audience's needs first. By understanding their preferences, providing value, and delivering content in an appealing and accessible format, you can capture their attention and build a loyal following.

Chapter 7: Optimizing Search Engine Visibility and Search Engine Marketing

You are not alone. You're competing in a crowded global space, so you need to do all you can to get close to the top in the search engine results. Whomever joked that the best place to hide a body in on page three of a Google search was rather astute.

Financial services companies can optimize their search engine visibility and utilize search engine marketing through the following strategies:

Search Engine Optimization (SEO):
- Conduct keyword research to identify relevant keywords and phrases that your target audience is searching for.
- Optimize your website's meta tags, headings, and content with targeted keywords but don't overdo it or you'll risk bot boycott. Since these algorithms change often, it's best to consult an SEO expert about current best practices.
- Create high-quality, informative, and engaging content that aligns with user intent and addresses their search queries.
- Optimize your website's loading speed, mobile responsiveness, and overall user experience. It aggravates people when websites aren't optimized for mobile.
- Build high-quality backlinks from reputable and relevant websites to improve your website's authority and visibility. If this sounds like a foreign language, hire an expert.
- Utilize local SEO strategies, such as optimizing for location-based keywords and claiming your business listing on Google My Business.

Content Marketing:
- Develop a content marketing strategy that includes blog articles, whitepapers, videos, infographics, or podcasts targeting relevant financial topics and keywords. Be sure to also develop a sensible deployment calendar to keep it all on track.
- Produce valuable and informative content that educates and engages your audience, positioning your brand as a trusted resource.
- Promote your content through social media channels, email newsletters, and industry forums to expand its reach and visibility. You might be surprised how many different ways you can use the same (or some portion of) materials you've created from scratch.
- Incorporate internal linking within your content to guide users to relevant pages on your website. Make it easy for people to find things.

Pay-Per-Click Advertising (PPC):
- Utilize search engine advertising platforms like Google Ads or Bing Ads to create targeted PPC campaigns.
- Conduct keyword research to identify relevant keywords with high search volume and reasonable competition. Note the term reasonable. Don't blow the budget on one keyword, no matter how enticing it may be.

- Develop compelling ad copy that highlights your unique value proposition, represents your brand's tone and style, and encourages clicks.
- Optimize your landing pages to align with your ad copy and provide a clear call-to-action. People should always know they're still beneath your brand umbrella.
- Continuously monitor and optimize your PPC campaigns based on performance metrics such as click-through rates, conversion rates, and return on ad expenditure.

Local Search Optimization:
- Optimize your business listings on local directories, such as Google My Business, Yelp, and industry-specific directories.
- Ensure your business name, address, and phone number (NAP) are correct and consistent across all directories.
- Encourage satisfied clients to leave positive reviews on your business listings, as they can influence your search visibility and reputation.

Social Media Marketing:
- Maintain an active presence on social media platforms relevant to your target audience.
- Share informative content, industry insights, and updates on your social media channels.
- Engage with your audience by responding to comments, messages, and inquiries in a timely manner.
- Utilize social media advertising to target specific demographics, promote your services or content, and drive organic traffic to your website.

Analytics and Optimization:
- Use web analytics tools, such as Google Analytics, to track and analyze your website's performance, user behavior, and conversion metrics.
- Monitor keyword rankings, website traffic, bounce rates, and conversion rates to identify areas for improvement.
- Adjust your SEO and marketing strategies based on the data and insights gathered from all analytics sources.

By implementing these strategies, financial marketers can enhance their organization's search engine visibility, attract relevant traffic, and increase their online presence. It's important to continuously monitor and adapt your strategies to stay ahead in the competitive online landscape.

Laws/Rules/Regulatory considerations for online marketing

In the United States, there are regulatory rules and guidelines that govern the marketing of financial services. These regulations aim to protect consumers, ensure fair competition, and maintain the integrity of the financial industry. Though it is strongly recommended that your firm's lawyers and compliance professionals are consulted before the launch of any marketing activities, here are some key regulations to keep top of mind:

Truth in Lending Act (TILA):
- TILA requires lenders and financial institutions to disclose important terms and costs associated with consumer credit transactions.
- Online marketing materials for loans, credit cards, and other consumer credit products must provide clear and accurate information about interest rates, fees, repayment terms, and other relevant details.

Equal Credit Opportunity Act (ECOA):
- ECOA prohibits discrimination in any aspect of a credit transaction, including marketing.
- Financial institutions must ensure that their online marketing practices do not discriminate against individuals based on factors such as race, gender, age, or marital status.

Consumer Financial Protection Bureau (CFPB) Regulations:
- The CFPB enforces various regulations to protect consumers in the financial industry.
- This includes rules under the Truth in Advertising Act and the Consumer Financial Protection Act, which regulate the content and practices of financial service providers in their online marketing efforts.

Securities and Exchange Commission (SEC) Regulations:
- The SEC regulates the marketing and sale of securities, investment products, and financial services.
- Firms offering investment opportunities must comply with regulations such as the Securities Act of 1933 and the Investment Advisers Act of 1940, which govern the content and distribution of online marketing materials.

Federal Trade Commission (FTC) Regulations:
- The FTC regulates advertising and marketing practices across various industries, including financial services.
- Financial institutions must comply with regulations such as the FTC Act, which prohibits deceptive or unfair advertising practices.

Gramm-Leach-Bliley Act (GLBA):
- GLBA requires financial institutions to protect the privacy and security of customers' personal information.
- Financial service providers must ensure that their online marketing activities adhere to data privacy requirements and provide clear disclosures about data collection and usage.

It's important to understand and comply with these regulations to avoid legal and regulatory issues. Non-compliance can result in penalties, legal action, reputational damage, and loss of consumer trust. It is advisable to consult legal and compliance professionals to ensure that your firm's online marketing practices align with the applicable regulations.

Incorporating mobile marketing and app development strategies

Everyone is on the go. To meet customers where they are, financial services companies should consider incorporating mobile marketing and app development strategies to engage effectively and provide convenient access.

Mobile-Friendly Website: Ensure your website is mobile-friendly, responsive, and optimized for mobile viewing. Test, test, test. How annoying is it when features should be there but aren't, or they're there, but don't work right? Don't be that company. Your customers' mobile use should provide a seamless browsing experience, easy navigation, and quick access to important information and services. In other words, it should work.

Mobile Apps: Develop a proprietary mobile app that offers valuable features and services to your customers. Consider functionalities like account management, transaction history, fund transfers, financial tools, and personalized notifications. Focus on usability, security, and a user-friendly interface.

Personalized Messaging: Use mobile marketing channels like SMS and push notifications to deliver personalized messages to your customers. But don't overdo it. Your customers may like you, but they still don't want you texting them all the time. Be judicious and tailor your messages based on their preferences, behavior, and transaction history. Use these channels to share relevant offers, reminders, alerts, and important updates.

Location-Based Services: Leverage location-based technology to offer targeted services and promotions. For example, provide personalized recommendations, nearby branch or ATM locations, or special offers based on the user's geographic location.

Mobile Payments: Incorporate mobile payment options into your app or mobile website. Offer convenient and secure payment methods like mobile wallets or peer-to-peer payment services. It is imperative that you ensure compliance with relevant payment industry standards and security protocols.

App Store Optimization (ASO): Optimize your mobile app's visibility in app stores by utilizing ASO techniques. This includes optimizing your app title, description, keywords, and visuals to improve discoverability and attract relevant users. Market your app to market yourself.

User Experience (UX) Design: Focus on delivering a seamless and intuitive user experience across your mobile platforms. Conduct user testing, gather feedback, and iterate on your app's design to ensure it meets the needs and preferences of your target audience. If you modify something based on customer feedback, let users know you've been motivated to do so. This simple act will encourage more feedback, more engagement, and more respect for the customer-centricity of your brand.

Mobile Advertising: Implement mobile advertising campaigns to reach a wider audience. Consider utilizing mobile ad networks, social media platforms, and programmatic advertising to target specific demographics and promote your services.

Mobile Analytics: Implement mobile analytics tools to track user behavior, engagement, and conversion metrics within your mobile app. Gain insights into user preferences, popular features, and areas for improvement. Use this data to refine your mobile marketing strategies.

Compliance and Security: Ensure that your mobile marketing and app development strategies comply with or even exceed relevant regulatory guidelines and industry best practices. Implement robust security measures to protect customer data and maintain trust.

By incorporating mobile marketing and app development strategies, financial services companies can enhance customer engagement, deliver personalized experiences, and provide convenient access to their services. It's crucial to stay updated with the latest mobile trends, monitor user feedback, and continuously refine your mobile strategies to meet evolving customer expectations.

Chapter 8: Harnessing the Power of Content Marketing

In today's digital landscape, content marketing has emerged as a powerful tool for financial services firms to connect with their audience, build trust, and drive business growth. With the increasing competition and changing consumer behavior, traditional marketing approaches alone may no longer be sufficient. That's where content marketing comes into play, offering a strategic approach to engage, educate, and inspire target audiences in the financial industry.

Content marketing involves creating and distributing valuable, relevant, and consistent content to attract and retain a clearly defined audience. It goes beyond promotional messages and instead focuses on delivering informative, educational, and entertaining content that resonates with the needs and interests of the target market. **You become more than a product: you become a resource.** By harnessing the power of content marketing, financial services firms can establish thought leadership, strengthen their brand, and foster meaningful customer relationships.

One of the key advantages of content marketing in the financial services industry is its ability to provide value-added information. Financial decisions can be complex, and consumers often seek guidance and knowledge (sometimes from multiple sources) to make informed choices. By producing high-quality content that addresses common financial concerns, offers insights, and simplifies complex and often intimidating concepts, financial services firms can position themselves as trusted advisors and industry experts. This is not a sell, sell, sell strategy.

Used well, a strong content strategy helps brands engage with their audience at various stages of the customer journey. Through blog articles, videos, podcasts, infographics, and social media posts, firms can attract potential customers, nurture leads, and support existing clients. By consistently delivering valuable content, financial services firms can build brand awareness, credibility, and loyalty, fostering long-term relationships with their audience—and the sphere of people that primary audience may influence.

That influence is considered an amplification of your brand's reach and visibility. In today's digital age, consumers actively seek information online, including through influencers, making search engines and social media platforms primary sources of research and discovery. By optimizing content and strategically promoting (or being organically promoted by others), financial services firms can expand their reach, attract relevant traffic, and increase their online visibility.

By leveraging analytics tools, firms can track content performance, measure engagement metrics, and gain insights into customer preferences and behavior. This data-driven approach enables firms to refine their content strategies, target specific customer segments, and continually improve their marketing efforts.

Connect with your target audience, build trust, and differentiate your business in a crowded marketplace through your content. By becoming valuable and relevant, firms can establish thought leadership, drive brand engagement, and nurture lasting relationships that can convert prospects into sales. With its ability to educate, inform, and inspire, content marketing is a powerful tool that can help firms navigate the ever-changing landscape and achieve sustainable long-term growth.

Understanding the role of content marketing in financial services

Content marketing plays a crucial role in financial marketing in seven important ways:

1. Educating and Informing
Financial services can be complex, and consumers often require guidance and information to make informed decisions. Content marketing is an opportunity to create educational and informative content that simplifies intimidating concepts, addresses common financial concerns, and empowers customers with knowledge. By providing valuable insights and resources, firms establish themselves as trustworthy and position their brand as a reliable.

2. Establishing Thought Leadership
Content marketing allows financial services firms to showcase their expertise and industry knowledge. By sharing insights, market trends, and thought-provoking content, firms can demonstrate their insight which enhances their reputation, builds credibility, and attracts potential clients who are seeking expert guidance. Thought leadership content can take the form of blog articles, whitepapers, research reports, webinars, and industry commentary. Podcasts have emerged as wonderful and engaging thought-leadership options on wide-ranging topics, and are often consumable on the go.

3. Building Trust and Relationships
If the point hasn't been driven home yet, I'll reiterate that trust is a vital component in the financial services industry. Through content marketing, firms can cultivate trust by consistently delivering what the audience wants, but also what they haven't even yet considered. By proactively addressing customer pain points, offering solutions, and sharing real-life examples, firms establish themselves as partners in their customers' success. Over time, this trust translates into stronger relationships, customer loyalty, and increased business opportunities.

4. Nurturing Leads and Conversions
Content marketing enables financial services firms to nurture leads throughout the customer journey. When a prospect first meets a brand, they may not need the brand's services. By creating content tailored to specific stages of the buying process, firms can engage prospects, provide relevant information, and cultivate ongoing relationships so when they do eventually need the brand's service, the relationship has already been established and solidified. Blog posts and educational videos can attract potential customers, while case studies and client testimonials can help convert leads into clients.

Effective content marketing nurtures prospects and guides them toward making informed decisions.

5.   Enhancing Brand Awareness and Visibility
Content marketing is a powerful tool for boosting brand awareness and expanding reach. By creating valuable content that is optimized for search engines, firms can organically improve their visibility in online search results. Social media platforms also offer opportunities to promote content and reach a broader audience. Sharing valuable content consistently helps financial services firms stay top-of-mind with their target audience, increasing brand recall and recognition.

6.   Engaging through Various Channels
Content marketing enables financial services firms to engage customers through various channels and formats. This includes blog posts, articles, videos, podcasts, infographics, social media posts, and email newsletters. By diversifying content formats and distribution channels, firms can cater to different customer preferences and reach audiences across multiple touchpoints. When your brand seems to "be everywhere", it garners subconscious respect from prospective clients.

7.   Measuring and Iterating
Content marketing provides valuable insights through analytics and data tracking. Financial services firms can measure content performance, engagement metrics, and conversion rates to gain insights into customer preferences, behavior, and, most importantly, content effectiveness. These insights help firms refine their content strategies, identify opportunities for improvement, and create more impactful content over time.

Fresh, useful and informative content is always welcome in the over-crowded market of regurgitated ideas. Your content strategy should first aim to be relevant and helpful well before you attempt to sell anything. Eventually, you'll solidify a position of expertise in the mind of your key audience and they'll seek you out as an authority on a topic. Keep bringing value and people will learn to trust and connect with your brand—and prospects will become clients.

So how do you create the best content for your target audience?

Creating valuable and relevant content is essential. Getting it done takes some consideration and planning. Start with these useful tips:

Know Your Audience: When you know exactly whom you should be talking to (demographics, preferences, needs, obstacles, etc.) it will help you develop buyer personas to represent your ideal customers and their specific challenges. This knowledge will guide your content creation process and help you tailor content to address their specific needs.

Address Common Pain Points: Identify the common pain points and challenges faced by your target audience. Create content that addresses these pain points head-on, so they don't feel alone in their confusion or hesitation. Then, offers practical solutions and provide actionable advice. This could include articles, guides, videos, or case studies that address topics like budgeting, saving, investing, retirement planning, or debt management. By admitting to the audience that a topic is hard, confusing or strange, you humanize your company and show empathy to your audience.

Provide Education and Insights: Financial services firms have deep industry knowledge that can be valuable. Share educational content that explains complex financial concepts in simple terms. Offer insights into market trends, regulatory changes, or investment strategies. Consider creating how-to guides, tutorials, or explainer videos that empower your audience to make informed financial decisions. And change it up: mix and match topics, lengths, and formats.

Leverage Customer Stories and Testimonials: Real-life stories and testimonials from satisfied clients can be powerful in showcasing the impact of your services. Feature case studies or success stories that highlight how your financial solutions have helped actual individuals or real-world businesses achieve their goals. These stories provide social proof and build credibility for your brand.

Stay Updated with Industry News: Stay abreast of the latest industry news, trends, and developments. Share your perspectives on relevant news articles or provide commentary on financial events even if (especially if) your take departs from the mainstream. This demonstrates your expertise and keeps your audience informed about the latest happenings in the financial world.

Use Visuals and Infographics: Visual content such as infographics, charts, and diagrams can make complex financial information more digestible and engaging. Use visual elements to enhance the understanding of your content and make it aesthetically appealing. Visuals can help convey information quickly and attract the attention of your audience.

Encourage Interactivity and Engagement: Foster engagement by incorporating interactive elements into your content. This can include quizzes, polls, surveys, or interactive calculators that allow users to assess their financial situation or make informed decisions. Encourage your audience to comment, share their thoughts, ask questions, and be responsive in your interactions.

Tailor Content Formats to Preferences: Consider the preferences and habits of your target audience when choosing content formats. Some may prefer reading blog articles, while others may prefer watching videos or listening to podcasts. Diversify your content formats to cater to different preferences and provide options that align with how your audience consumes information. Remember, one piece of content may be used in several ways, so be efficient!

Seek Feedback and Listen to Your Audience: Actively seek feedback from your audience to understand their needs, preferences, and objections. This can be done through surveys, social media interactions, or direct communication. Use this feedback to refine your content strategy and create content that truly resonates with your audience.

By implementing these strategies, financial firms can create consistently fresh and impactful content that won't bore audiences to sleep, inundate them with useless spam, or be worthless in their pursuit of reliable, trustworthy information. Gain your audience's trust. Gain your audience's confidence. Gain your audience's business.

Developing thought leadership through long form content

Whitepapers, articles, and in-depth blog posts are a powerful trilogy of financial services content options. Since they are not geared to be witty, pithy or confined by a character count, their use enables thought leadership that delves deeper into a topic for a more comprehensive understanding of important elements. To support long form tactics such as these, you need enough insight and information to make it worthwhile. Don't waste people's time. If it's going to be long, it had better be chock-full of great information. To build out content that tells a compelling story, use the following:

In-Depth Research and Analysis
Conduct proprietary research on industry trends, market insights, or specific financial topics relevant to your target audience. Use this research to provide unique insights, analysis, and data-backed perspectives in your whitepapers, articles, and blog posts. Present information that goes beyond surface-level and offers valuable, in-depth analysis that can't be found elsewhere.

Address Current Industry Challenges
Identify the pressing challenges faced by your target audience or the financial industry as a whole. Create content that offers practical solutions, actionable advice, and innovative

strategies to overcome these challenges. Share your unique expertise and provide sound guidance that helps your audience navigate (or consider) complex financial issues.

Thought-Provoking Content
Develop thought-provoking content that challenges conventional wisdom, offers new perspectives, or introduces innovative approaches. Share your vision for the future of the financial industry and discuss emerging trends or disruptive technologies. By pushing the boundaries of conventional thinking, you position yourself as a forward-thinking leader in the field. When your theories or insights prove out, you garner immediate deference. (When they don't, publish a piece on that as well and do a post-mortem about why. This level of humility and accountability will make you even more credible.)

Case Studies and Success Stories
Highlight real-world examples of how your work has made a positive impact on your clients' lives or businesses. Showcase case studies and success stories that demonstrate the tangible results achieved through your expertise and services. These stories provide valuable social proof that you can perform as promised, and as such they build trust among your audience.

Collaborate for Impact
Collaborate with other experts, influencers, or thought leaders in the financial or financial-adjacent industries. Co-author whitepapers, contribute to joint articles or participate in panel discussions. By associating your brand with respected individuals or organizations, you enhance your credibility and expand your reach to new audiences. Be smart about who you align with.

Engage in Industry Events and Conferences
Participate in relevant industry events, conferences, or webinars as a speaker, panelist, or moderator. Share your knowledge, insights, and expertise with the audience. Such appearances establish you as an authoritative voice in the industry and provide networking opportunities to connect with other thought leaders. In other words, be in the room where it happens.

Foster a Strong Online Presence
Consistently publish high-quality content on your website's blog or through guest contributions on reputable industry publications for cross promotion. Share your content across social media platforms and engage in meaningful discussions with your audience. Encourage comments, questions, and shares to foster engagement and expand your reach.

Provide Actionable and Practical Advice
Your thought leadership content should offer useful advice that your audience can implement in their financial endeavors. Audiences enjoy step-by-step guides, checklists, or templates that help them take actual action. By delivering value this way, you position yourself as a trustworthy guide.

Continuously Learn and Stay Updated
Stay abreast of the latest trends, regulatory changes, and advancements in the financial industry. Invest time in continuous learning to stay ahead of the curve. Be curious, and never rest on your laurels. Share your knowledge and insights through informative content that educates and empowers.

Promote Your Content
Effective promotion is essential to ensure your two cents reach a wide audience. Leverage social media channels, email newsletters, and professional networks to share your content with relevant communities. Collaborate with industry influencers or media outlets to amplify your reach.

Following all or some of the strategies above can help firms develop a substantial following. Deep and unique insights shared through whitepapers, articles, and blog posts will be received as valuable offerings. Addressing industry challenges and providing practical guidance, can establish your brand as a trusted authority in the space, attracting clients and fostering long-term relationships.

Distributing and promoting all that digital content

Implementing effective distribution and promotion strategies is crucial ensure the digital content reaches and engages the actual target audience. To do this effectively and efficiently, you'll need to consider the following:

Define Your Distribution Channels
Identify the most relevant channels to reach your target audience. This could include your website, blog, social media platforms, email newsletters, industry publications (traditional route), or content syndication platforms. Focus on channels that align with your audience's preferences and behavior. It's better to do a few things well than everything haphazardly.

Optimize Your Website
Ensure your website is user-friendly, visually appealing, and optimized for search engines and for mobile. Publish your content on your website's blog and make it easily accessible for visitors. Use effective SEO strategies, such as incorporating relevant keywords and optimizing meta tags, to improve search engine visibility.

Leverage Social Media
Utilize social media platforms such as LinkedIn, X (formerly Twitter), Facebook, or Instagram to distribute and promote your content. Create engaging social media posts that include snippets or excerpts from your content, along with compelling visuals. Whet their appetite. Then, engage with your audience, respond to comments, and actively share and reshare your content across platforms.

Email Marketing
Build an email subscriber list and leverage it to distribute your content directly to interested individuals. Scrub it regularly so it's not full of dead leads. Be sure to segment your email list based on interests or demographics to send targeted content to specific audiences. Craft attention-grabbing (and short) subject lines, and personalize the email content to increase open rates and engagement. Take these two options:

      A. Learn whether your portfolio is optimized to meet your retirement goals
      B. 5 ways to check portfolio efficiency

Which do you find more engaging? Shorter, actionable headlines get more clicks. A/B test your ideas, then track, track, track. If something's not working, kill it and move on. Never marry yourself to your content (especially your headlines).

Content Syndication
Consider syndicating your content on relevant industry platforms, publications, or content aggregators. This helps expand your reach to new audiences and establishes your brand as an intelligent leader. Be selective with syndication platforms, ensuring they align with your target audience and maintain a high-quality standard.

Collaborate with Influencers
Identify influencers, experts, or industry leaders in the financial services space who have a strong following and impeccable credibility. Collaborate with them to co-create content, share insights, or participate in interviews or webinars. Leveraging their influence can significantly expand the reach and credibility of your content.

*A word about interviews and podcasts: be sure that your firm's representative matches or at least paces with the energy of the influencer. There's nothing more uncomfortable than a mismatch of energy levels that can make your ambassador seem dull, stuffy, or obtuse. Send someone charismatic. Bonus points if they're quick-witted and have a sense of humor.

Guest Posting and Contributed Articles
Seek opportunities to contribute guest posts or articles to reputable industry publications, blogs, or websites. This helps you tap into existing audiences and positions your brand as an authority. Follow the guidelines provided by each publication and ensure your content provides unique value to their readers.

Paid Advertising
Consider paid advertising channels such as Google Ads, social media advertising, or sponsored content to boost the visibility and reach of your content. Target specific keywords, demographics, or interests to ensure your content reaches the right audience. Monitor and optimize your campaigns to maximize results.

Keep in mind that average click-through rates aren't exactly high. For Google Ads, you're looking at a click-through-rate (CTR) of about 1-2% for top positions. Facebook ads are usually just under 1% unless they're very well-optimized. Email marketing tends to have open rates between 15 – 25%, but the actual CTR can be as low as 2-3% unless it's very well targeted, timely, and relevant. So, be smart about where and how you spend your time and dollars.

Cross-Promotion and Internal Linking
Promote your content across different channels by cross-linking related articles, blog posts, or resources. Include links to relevant content within your own website to guide visitors to explore more of your content, and make sure to monitor for dead links. This improves the user experience and increases the visibility of your content.

Track and Analyze Performance
Use analytics tools to monitor the performance of your content distribution efforts. Track metrics such as website traffic, engagement, social media interactions, email open rates, and

conversions. Analyze the data to identify what channels and content types are resonating most with your audience. Make adjustments as needed. Do more of what works, and less of what doesn't for the best return on your investment.

Remember, content distribution and promotion require consistency, quality, and a deep understanding of your target audience. By implementing these strategies and continually optimizing your approach, you can effectively distribute and promote your content, reaching and engaging your intended audience in ways that impact their perception of your brand.

10 Point CHECKLIST for Smart Content Marketing

1. Define Clear Objectives:
    a. Identify the goals and objectives of your content marketing strategy.
    b. Ensure they align with your overall marketing and business objectives. Examples: Increase brand awareness, generate leads, drive website traffic, educate and engage the target audience.

2. Understand Your Target Audience:
    a. Conduct thorough market research to understand your audience's needs, preferences, and pain points.
    b. Develop detailed buyer personas to guide your content creation process.
    c. Segment your audience based on demographics, interests, and behaviors for targeted content delivery.

3. Develop a Content Plan:
    a. Create an editorial calendar outlining content topics, formats, and publishing schedule.
    b. Consider the buyer's journey and create content that aligns with each stage (awareness, consideration, decision).
    c. Balance educational, informative, and promotional content to provide value to your audience.

4. Craft Compelling and Valuable Content:
    a. Create high-quality content that is engaging, informative, and relevant to your audience.
    b. Incorporate different formats such as blog posts, articles, videos, infographics, eBooks, and case studies.
    c. Ensure content is well-researched, properly structured, and written in a clear and concise manner.

5. Optimize for Search Engines:
    a. Conduct keyword research to identify relevant keywords and incorporate them naturally into your content.
    b. Optimize meta tags, headings, and URLs for search engine visibility.
    c. Use internal and external links to enhance SEO and provide additional value to readers.

6. Promote Your Content:
    a. Develop a distribution plan to reach your target audience effectively.
    b. Leverage social media channels, email marketing, influencer partnerships, and online communities to promote your content.

c. Consider paid advertising, such as PPC campaigns or sponsored content, to extend your reach.

7. Measure and Analyze:
    a. Define key performance indicators (KPIs) to track the success of your content marketing efforts.
    b. Use web analytics tools to measure metrics like website traffic, engagement, conversion rates, and social media metrics.
    c. Regularly analyze the data to identify trends, assess performance, and make data-driven decisions for improvement.

8. Iterate and Improve:
    a. Continuously review and refine your content strategy based on data insights and audience feedback.
    b. Stay updated on industry trends and adjust your approach accordingly.
    c. Experiment with new content formats and distribution channels to optimize your strategy over time.

9. Nurture Audience Engagement:
    a. Encourage comments, shares, and discussions around your content.
    b. Respond to audience inquiries and feedback promptly.
    c. Foster a sense of community by engaging with your audience on social media platforms and through email communications.

10. Monitor and Adapt:
    a. Stay informed about changes in the industry, audience preferences, and content consumption habits.
    b. Continuously monitor the performance of your content and adapt your strategy as needed.
    c. Stay agile and be willing to experiment with new approaches to keep your content marketing strategy effective.

By following this checklist, you can develop and execute a smart content marketing strategy that engages your target audience, drives results, and contributes to the growth and success of your business.

SAMPLE Content Marketing Calendar

Here is a sample content marketing schedule to help illustrate the different components and how they can work in harmony. It can be adjusted and expanded based on your specific content marketing goals, target audience, and resources.

Remember to maintain **consistency** in content delivery and engage with your audience regularly to build a strong online presence and drive meaningful interactions.

Month: June
Content Themes: Retirement Planning, Investment Strategies

Week 1:

Blog Post: "5 Essential Retirement Planning Tips for Every Age Group"

Social Media: Share blog post on LinkedIn, X (formerly Twitter), and Facebook with engaging captions and relevant hashtags.

Email Newsletter: Send a newsletter to subscribers with highlights from the blog post and additional retirement planning resources such as an online calculator.

Week 2:

Social Media Part 1: Share the video on YouTube and promote it on other social media channels. (Video: "Introduction to Investment Strategies: A Beginner's Guide")

Social Media Part 2: Share this infographic on Instagram and Pinterest with engaging captions. (Infographic: "The Power of Diversification: Building a Balanced Investment Portfolio")

Week 3:

Case Study: "Client Success Story: How Our Investment Strategy Helped Sarah Get Her PhD "

Social Media: Share snippets and key takeaways from the case study on LinkedIn and X (formerly Twitter).

Guest Blog Post: Collaborate with a reputable finance blogger on a guest post about investment trends in the education savings market.

Social Media: Share the guest post on LinkedIn and Facebook, giving credit to the guest blogger.

Week 4:

Webinar: "Planning for Retirement: Strategies for a Secure Financial Future"

Social Media: Promote the webinar on all platforms and encourage registrations.

Email Campaign: Send a dedicated email to your subscriber list inviting them to join the webinar.

Blog Post: "Top Investment Opportunities in the Current Economic Climate"

Social Media: Share the blog post on LinkedIn, X (formerly Twitter), and Facebook.

Ongoing:

Social Media Engagement: Regularly engage with followers by responding to comments, sharing relevant industry news, and posing questions to encourage conversations.

Content Repurposing: Repurpose existing content into different formats such as videos, infographics, and podcasts to reach a wider audience.

Monitor Analytics: Continuously monitor and analyze website traffic, social media metrics, and email engagement to track the performance of your content and make data-driven decisions for improvement.

Chapter 9: Relationship Marketing

Engaging with clients through relationship marketing involves building and nurturing long-term connections based on trust, personalized exchanges, and ongoing communication. It goes beyond transactional interactions and focuses on creating meaningful bonds. Here are some key aspects of engaging with clients through relationship marketing:

Personalized Communication
Relationship marketing emphasizes understanding and catering to the individual needs and preferences of each client. Financial services firms should gather relevant client information and use it to personalize communication, whether it's through email, phone calls, or in-person meetings. A comprehensive customer relationship management (CRM) tool is key as it will help you tailor messages, offers, and recommendations to align with clients' specific goals, circumstances, and interests. They'll feel known and seen, and therefore immediately more comfortable with your brand.

Building Trust and Credibility
Trust is a must. Relationship marketing plays a crucial role. Firms should prioritize transparency, integrity, and delivering on promises. An often overlooked, but extremely valuable part of building trust, is admitting when you make a mistake. Trying to sweep it under the rug builds distrust, while copping to it with an apology gives the impression of transparency and humanness. So if you mess up, fess up.

Proactive Relationship Management
Relationship marketing needs to be proactive rather than reactive. Regularly reach out to clients to check in, provide updates, and offer relevant insights or opportunities. Anticipating clients' needs and being motivated to address them demonstrates care and commitment to their financial well-being.

Value-Added Services and Education
Relationship marketing goes beyond selling financial products or services. It focuses on providing value-added services and educational resources to clients and, hopefully, their families for generations to come. This can include hosting educational webinars, organizing workshops, or sharing informative content through newsletters or blog posts. By empowering clients with knowledge and helping them make informed decisions, firms strengthen the client-advisor relationship. You must trust them to use the information well: they must trust you to provide information that helps them stay informed.

Timely and Responsive Support
Being responsive to client inquiries, concerns, and feedback is crucial for effective relationship marketing. Financial services firms should strive to provide timely and accurate support, addressing client needs promptly. Responsiveness builds confidence and reassures clients that

their concerns are heard and valued. No one wants to scream into the void. Be there for them, as a human.

Relationship-Building Events and Networking
Hosting client appreciation events, networking opportunities, or exclusive gatherings can help develop stronger relationships. These events create chances for clients to connect with each other and with representatives from your organization. By facilitating networking and social interactions, firms deepen client relationships and create a sense of belonging.

Continuous Relationship Monitoring
Relationship marketing requires ongoing monitoring and evaluation of client relationships. Regularly assess client satisfaction, gather feedback, and identify areas for improvement. Utilizing a good CRM can help track interactions, preferences, and communication history to ensure personalized and informed engagement. Know where you stand. Fix what can be improved. Share how well you've listened and how valuable the client's feedback was to your improvement.

Referral and Loyalty Programs
Encouraging client referrals and rewarding loyalty can further strengthen relationships. Implement referral programs that incentivize clients to refer friends and family. Recognize and reward loyal clients through exclusive offers, discounts, or personalized benefits. These programs not only foster client engagement but also help expand the firm's client base.

Embracing Technology
Leverage technology to enhance relationship marketing efforts. Digital platforms, customer portals, and mobile apps can provide convenient access to information, account management tools, and personalized insights. Embracing technology enables seamless communication and engagement across multiple channels, catering to clients' preferences and enhancing their overall user experience.

By adopting and committing to relationship marketing strategies, firms can deepen client engagement, foster trust and loyalty, and differentiate themselves in a competitive industry. Strong, lasting relationships with clients can lead to increased client satisfaction, higher retention rates, and positive referrals, ultimately driving business growth and success. It costs far more to find new clients than to keep existing ones. In life and business, be sure to keep your relationships strong.

Establishing and nurturing client relationships in 11 steps

1. Keep the communications as personalized as possible using a good CRM.
2. Regularly engage and provide updates on their accounts and the industry
3. Offer value-added services like exclusive events or access
4. Provide exceptional, professional, and responsive customer service
5. Demonstrate expertise and thought leadership by publishing prolifically
6. Show face by participating in interviews, events, and conferences
7. Seek client feedback to ensure satisfaction and improve where possible
8. Foster personal connections by having a genuine rapport with customers
9. Leverage technology and digital tools for enhanced convenience
10. Continuously adapt and innovate in an ever-changing marketplace
11. Encourage referrals and advocacy from happy clients

It's a marathon, not a sprint, when it comes to nurturing client relationships. Allow it to become part of your standard operating practices, not just an "activity" done when the numbers sag.

By consistently implementing these strategies, financial services firms can establish and nurture strong client relationships, fostering loyalty, trust, and long-term partnerships. Remember, building client relationships requires consistent effort, open communication, and a client-centric approach to deliver value and exceed expectations.

Effective client communication and engagement

If it's not effective, it's not worth the effort. How can you communicate most effectively with clients?

1. Be clear and transparent: Use understandable and concise language, avoiding jargon and complex terms. You're not trying to prove your intelligence; you're trying to get your point across effectively. Also, be transparent about fees, charges, and the risks associated with financial products or services. Review your statements and reports to see if they're cluttered and confusing. Improve them if possible so clients can quickly see how their investments are performing.

2. Update regularly: Provide clients with regular updates on their accounts, investment performance, and market trends. Send periodic statements, performance reports, or newsletters to keep clients informed and engaged. Wherever possible, use visual aids, charts, or infographics so the information is easily digestible.

3. Employ various channels: Communicate in multiple ways. Some people may prefer email updates, while others may prefer phone calls or in-person meetings. Employ technology to create and maintain client portals or mobile apps that give clients access to their account information and enable secure communication.

4. Be proactive in your outreach: Don't wait for clients to reach out to you. Share insights or discuss changes in the market before you're asked. Reach out during important milestones, to show your attention and care. Insist on regular maintenance check-ins.

5. Educate and guide: Offer educational resources and guidance to empower clients in making informed financial decisions. Develop materials, webinars, or workshops on topics relevant to their goals. Provide personalized financial planning services and offer recommendations aligned with their objectives.

6. Individualized service: Financial services is a personal business. Take the time to understand a person's goals, preferences, and risk tolerance. Then tailor your recommendations and communication to their unique situation. Address clients by preferred name and remember important details they share about their financial situation or personal life. Put it all in the CRM.

7. Be responsive: Being prompt and responsive is the cost of entry. Go further by having excellently trained customer-facing staff. Teach them to be patient, clear, helpful and empowered to go beyond in an effort to help clients feel valued and supported. Technology, such as chatbots or AI-powered assistants, are useful to provide instant responses and support when needed—especially after hours—but nothing is better than a competent human eager to help.

8. Connect with events: Organize client appreciation events, workshops, or seminars to support relationship-building and provide opportunities for networking—you with clients, and clients with other clients. These events create a mechanism for building sense of community and trust.

9. Ask how you're doing: Be prepared to not always like what you hear. However, negative feedback is incredibly useful to make you better. Use it. Surveys, focus groups and other organized market research activities have their place in the feedback process. But so does a casual question asked at the end of each client interaction, but be careful not to ask simple yes/no questions. Those aren't entirely helpful. Instead, ask, "What did we do well today?" and, "What could we have done better?" Actively listen to client feedback and thank them for providing it.

10. Stay current on industry changes: Finance is a dynamic industry with evolving regulations, market trends, and technological advancements. Stay updated on industry changes and communicate relevant updates to clients so they aren't blindsided. Connect what's happening on a national or international level to their own portfolio. All news is local.

Effective communication is a two-way process that involves active listening, responsiveness, and a client-centric approach to meet their needs and exceed expectations. Rather than speaking "at" your customers speak "with" them.

Implementing customer relationship management (CRM) systems

Customer relationship management (CRM) systems are more than a glorified phone book. They can greatly benefit financial services firms by streamlining processes, improving customer service, and enhancing client relationships. They are only as good as their maintenance, though.

If you use one or plan to, commit to regularly scrubbing it of outdated information so it can be a reliable daily resource for your team. If you already have one but it's not working up to its (or your) potential, consider these steps for a CRM audit to figure out if there's a better tool for your needs.

Define objectives and requirements
What do you want out of it? Clearly define your objectives for a CRM system. Identify the specific functionalities and features that will best support your business processes and client management. Determine the data you need to capture, track, and analyze to meet your goals. Be realistic about what you'll actually use; you don't necessarily need every bell and whistle. Let me rephrase that: you **definitely** don't need every bell and whistle and you won't use them all because there are only so many hours in a day, so don't pay for them (if you can avoid it).

Select the right CRM system
Research and evaluate CRM systems that align with your objectives and requirements. Consider factors such as scalability, user-friendliness, integration capabilities with other software, security features, and support services. Choose a CRM system that fits your firm's size, budget, and specific needs.

Customize and configure
Customize the CRM system to align with your firm's workflows, data structure, and terminology. It will become more "yours" as you use it. Configure the system to capture the necessary client data, such as contact information, account details, interaction history, and preferences. Above all, the system must allow for easy data entry, updates, and retrieval.

Data migration
If you have existing client data in spreadsheets or other systems, plan and execute a data migration process to transfer the data to the CRM system accurately. Scrub and format the data as needed to ensure data integrity and consistency.

User training and adoption
Provide comprehensive training to your staff on how to effectively use the CRM system. Train them on data entry, tracking interactions, generating reports, and leveraging the system's features to enhance client relationships. Encourage user adoption by highlighting the benefits and showing how the system simplifies their work. You may want to do this annually, as people tend to get into a rut or forget there are other features they aren't using.

Integration with Existing Systems
Integrate the CRM system with other existing systems in your firm, such as accounting software, portfolio management systems, or marketing automation tools. Seamless integration enables data synchronization and streamlines processes across different departments. Of course, you also want your system to be regularly backed up just in case there's a problem and a previous backup needs to be retrieved.

Develop Standard Processes
Define standardized processes for client management, lead generation, sales, and service delivery within the CRM system. Establish guidelines for capturing and updating client information, tracking interactions, assigning tasks, and managing workflows. Ensure that everyone follows these processes consistently to maintain data accuracy and provide consistent client experiences.

Data Security and Privacy
Implement robust security measures to protect client data and comply with privacy regulations, such as GDPR or CCPA. Encrypt sensitive data, restrict access based on user roles, and regularly review security protocols. Obtain client consent for data usage and communicate your privacy policies clearly.

Ongoing Maintenance and Support
Allocate resources for ongoing system maintenance, updates, and technical support. Regularly review and optimize the system's performance, address any issues, and incorporate user feedback for system improvements. Stay informed about updates and new features offered by the CRM vendor.

Continuous Improvement
Regularly assess the effectiveness of the CRM system in meeting your objectives. Gather feedback from users and clients to identify areas for improvement. Leverage the system's reporting and analytics capabilities to gain insights and make data-driven decisions to enhance client relationships.

CRM systems only work when they're put to work, and they work best when they're used regularly, uniformly across the firm, and with ease. Well done, a CRM system can provide a centralized view of client interactions, streamline processes, and enable personalized service, ultimately leading to stronger and more consistent client relationships and increased customer satisfaction.

Leveraging customer data for personalized marketing campaigns

Financial services firms can leverage customer data for personalized marketing campaigns by following certain practices and considering legal implications. Some points to consider:

1. Data collection and consent
   Ensure that you have proper consent from customers to collect and use their personal data for marketing purposes. Compliance with privacy regulations, such as the General Data Protection Regulation (GDPR) and the California Consumer Privacy Act (CCPA), is crucial. Clearly communicate your data collection practices, purpose, and any third-party involvement, and provide options for customers to opt-in or opt-out.

2. Data security and confidentiality
   Though this isn't a marketing function per se, data security is hugely important for financial services firms. As an organization, you should be committed to robust security measures to protect customer data from unauthorized access or breaches. Use encryption, firewalls, and access controls to safeguard data. Regularly review and update security protocols to stay ahead of evolving threats.

3. Data analytics, segmentation and personalized content
   Analytics and segmentation help you whittle your marketing lists into more focused groups so your messaging can have enhanced specificity. Demographics, preferences, behaviors, and transaction history help you continue to speak to customers' needs while

anticipating what might lay ahead. Identify patterns, trends, and insights to drive campaigns.

4. Marketing automation and CRM Integration
   Leverage marketing automation tools and integrate them with your customer relationship management (CRM) system. This allows for automated tracking of customer interactions, targeted messaging, and personalized follow-ups based on customer behavior or triggers.

5. Compliance with Marketing Regulations
   Stay compliant with marketing regulations specific to the financial services industry, such as those set forth by the Securities and Exchange Commission (SEC), Financial Industry Regulatory Authority (FINRA), and Consumer Financial Protection Bureau (CFPB). Adhere to rules regarding fair advertising, disclosure requirements, and prohibited practices.

6. Opt-Out and Privacy Preferences
   Provide customers with clear options to opt-out of receiving marketing communications or adjust their privacy preferences. Respect their choices and promptly honor any requests to opt-out. Make it easy for customers to manage their communication preferences through user-friendly interfaces or dedicated customer portals.

7. Customer Data Retention and Deletion
   Establish policies and procedures for data retention and deletion. Retain customer data only for as long as necessary and ensure secure deletion when it is no longer needed. Regularly review and update data retention practices to align with legal requirements.

8. Data Sharing and Third-Party Relationships
   Be transparent about data sharing practices with third-party vendors or partners. Ensure that they, too, have proper security measures in place and adhere to privacy regulations. Obtain necessary consent or agreements when sharing customer data, and conduct due diligence on the privacy practices of third parties.

9. Ongoing Compliance Monitoring
   Regularly review and monitor your marketing practices to ensure ongoing compliance with applicable regulations. Stay informed about changes in privacy laws and industry guidelines to make necessary adjustments.

Data, data everywhere. By following these practices and considering legal implications, financial services firms can effectively leverage customer data for personalized marketing campaigns while maintaining compliance with relevant regulations. It is crucial to prioritize data privacy and security, obtain proper consent, and provide customers with control over their personal information. Otherwise, your firm will seem risky, unprofessional, and even unscrupulous.

Chapter 10: Compliance and Ethical Considerations

In the US, adherence to compliance and ethical standards can't be overstated. These laws and guidelines help ensure that firms operate within the bounds of legal and regulatory frameworks while upholding uncompromising principles.

When you work in financial services marketing, the Compliance department becomes very familiar. They may be sticklers who throw a wrench in some of your most creative ideas, but they're in place to save you from regulatory hot water. Buy them a coffee or send them a holiday card. Their diligence protects you and the firm.

Here is an introduction to the complicated world of compliance and ethics in the financial services industry:

Compliance
Financial services firms are subject to a wide range of laws, regulations, and industry standards that govern their operations. Compliance involves adhering to these legal requirements to maintain the integrity of the financial system, protect consumers, and promote fair and transparent practices. Large financial services firms often have entire teams of compliance professionals tasked with protecting the firm from a public relations misstep, steep fines, or reputation-damaging litigation.

Key compliance areas for financial services firms may include:

Regulatory compliance
Firms must comply with regulations imposed by regulatory bodies such as the Securities and Exchange Commission (SEC), Financial Industry Regulatory Authority (FINRA), Consumer Financial Protection Bureau (CFPB), and various state regulatory agencies. These regulations address areas such as investor protection, market integrity, anti-money laundering, data privacy, and more.

Anti-money-laundering (AML) and know your customer (KYC)
Firms must implement robust AML and KYC programs to prevent money laundering, terrorist financing, and other illicit activities. This includes verifying customer identities, conducting due diligence, monitoring transactions, and reporting suspicious activities.

Data security and privacy
Firms must protect sensitive customer information and comply with data protection laws such as the Gramm-Leach-Bliley Act (GLBA) and state-level data breach notification laws. Safeguarding data through encryption, access controls, and regular security audits is essential.

Investor protection
Firms must provide fair and accurate information to investors, avoid misleading practices, and disclose potential risks associated with investments. They must also follow guidelines on suitability and fiduciary duty when providing investment advice.

Ethical Considerations
Ethics play a vital role in building trust, maintaining reputation, and fostering long-term relationships with clients. Financial services firms should uphold high ethical standards to ensure fair treatment of customers, transparent practices, and responsible conduct. Key ethical considerations for financial services firms include:

Conflicts of Interest
Firms should identify and manage conflicts of interest that could compromise the fair treatment of clients. This includes disclosing any potential conflicts and implementing policies to mitigate them. It's in a firm's best interest to proactively manage conflicts lest the press get a hold of something truly innocent that could be spun in unflattering and even damaging ways.

Fair and Responsible Lending
Firms engaged in lending activities should adhere to fair lending practices, ensuring equal access to credit and avoiding discriminatory practices. Responsible lending involves assessing borrowers' ability to repay and providing appropriate loan products absolutely blind of race, gender, national origin, sexual orientation, family status and other potentially discriminatory factors.

Transparency and disclosure
It is always a boon to conduct yourself honestly and in good faith. Firms should provide clear and understandable information to clients, ensuring transparency about fees, charges, risks, and terms of financial products and services. Full and accurate disclosure helps clients make informed decisions while keeping your credibility strong.

Professional Conduct
Employees and representatives of your organization should maintain professional conduct, integrity, and confidentiality. They should act in the best interests of clients, avoid deceptive practices, and adhere to ethical codes of conduct set by industry associations. It is also wise to limit the number of employees authorized to speak or post on behalf of your organization, and best to give those who do guardrails around your brand voice as well as proper media training.

Corporate Social Responsibility
Firms should consider their impact on society and the environment. Engaging in responsible business practices, supporting community initiatives, and promoting sustainable development may contribute to their overall ethical standing. It may be

prudent to steer clear of politically charged social issues lest you alienate a large swath of potential clients.

Compliance and ethical considerations are critical pillars of the financial services industry. Firms that prioritize compliance with laws and regulations, while adhering to ethical principles, are able to build trust, foster client loyalty, and contribute to the overall stability and integrity of the financial industry as a whole.

10 Ways to Stay Compliant Despite Ever-Changing Rules

1. Stay Informed: Keep up with the latest regulatory developments, changes in laws, and industry guidelines that apply to your specific area of financial services. Regularly review updates from regulatory bodies such as the Securities and Exchange Commission (SEC), Financial Industry Regulatory Authority (FINRA), and Consumer Financial Protection Bureau (CFPB).

2. Conduct Risk Assessments: Perform regular risk assessments to identify potential compliance risks within your operations. This includes evaluating areas such as data privacy and security, anti-money laundering (AML), know your customer (KYC), investor protection, and more. Assess the effectiveness of existing controls and develop mitigation strategies for identified risks.

3. Develop Compliance Programs: Establish comprehensive compliance programs that outline policies, procedures, and internal controls to ensure adherence to regulations. These programs should cover various aspects such as AML, KYC, privacy, cybersecurity, disclosure requirements, and customer protection. Include mechanisms for monitoring and reporting compliance violations or suspicious activities.

4. Training and Education: Provide ongoing training and education to employees on relevant compliance requirements and best practices. Ensure that employees understand their obligations, including ethical standards and regulatory obligations. Regular training sessions and updates can help keep employees informed and promote a culture of compliance.

5. Implement Internal Controls: Put in place robust internal controls to monitor and enforce compliance with regulations. This includes establishing segregation of duties, implementing approval processes, conducting periodic audits, and maintaining proper documentation. Internal controls should help identify and address any compliance gaps or violations.

6. Engage Compliance Officers: Designate compliance officers or teams responsible for overseeing compliance efforts within the organization. These individuals should have a deep understanding of applicable regulations and be well-versed in compliance best practices. They can provide guidance, conduct internal assessments, and ensure that compliance programs are effectively implemented.

7. Monitor Regulatory Updates: Stay proactive in monitoring regulatory updates and changes. Regularly review new regulations, guidelines, and enforcement actions issued by regulatory bodies. Stay engaged with industry associations, participate in forums and conferences, and network with peers to gain insights into emerging compliance trends or situations to look out for.

8. Establish Relationships with Regulators: Foster open communication and positive relationships with regulatory agencies. Be responsive to requests for information or examinations, and promptly address any identified compliance issues. Proactively engage with regulators to seek clarifications or guidance on compliance matters.

9. Conduct Independent Audits: Periodically engage external auditors or consultants to perform independent compliance audits. These audits help identify areas of non-compliance, assess the effectiveness of internal controls, and provide recommendations for improvement.

10. Regularly Review and Update Policies: Continuously review and update compliance policies and procedures to reflect changes in regulations, industry best practices, and emerging risks. Regularly communicate these updates to employees and ensure their understanding and adherence.

By adopting these practices, firms can establish a strong culture of compliance and ensure ongoing adherence to financial regulations and industry guidelines. Compliance should be treated as an integral part of business operations, with a commitment to ethical practices and the protection of clients' interests.

10 tips to maintain impeccable compliance

◊   Stay Informed of changes from regulatory bodies

◊   Conduct risk assessments regularly on security controls

◊   Develop compliance programs that cover policies, security, and reporting

◊   Train and educate all employees based on their roles and responsibilities

◊   Implement internal controls including periodic audits to identify weaknesses

◊   Engage experienced compliance officers to guide the firm and reduce exposure

◊   Monitor regulatory actions through industry and peer insights and trends

◊   Establish relationships with regulators for proactive clarification or guidance

◊   Conduct independent audits with external auditors to assess effectiveness

◊   Regularly review and update policies to reflect changes in the industry

Understanding privacy and data protection regulations

Privacy and data protection regulations for financial services firms in the US are designed to safeguard the personal information of clients and ensure responsible handling of data. The two key regulations that govern privacy and data protection are:

Gramm-Leach-Bliley Act (GLBA): The GLBA requires financial institutions to protect the privacy and confidentiality of client information. It imposes obligations on financial services firms to provide privacy notices to clients, implement safeguards to protect personal information, and restrict the sharing of non-public personal information with third parties unless authorized by the client.

California Consumer Privacy Act (CCPA): Although not specific to financial services, the CCPA has implications for financial institutions operating in California or dealing with California residents. It grants consumers certain rights over their personal information, such as the right to know what information is collected, the right to request deletion, and the right to opt-out of the sale of their personal information.

Other Regulations
In addition to these regulations, financial services firms must also comply with other relevant privacy and data protection laws at the federal and state levels, such as the Health Insurance Portability and Accountability Act (HIPAA) for health-related information and state-specific data breach notification laws.

To comply with privacy and data protection regulations, financial services firms should:

1. **Develop Privacy Policies:** Establish and communicate clear privacy policies that outline how personal information is collected, used, stored, and shared. Privacy policies should be easily accessible to clients and provide details on data handling practices.

2. **Implement Data Security Measures:** Put in place robust security measures to protect personal information from unauthorized access, use, or disclosure. This includes implementing strong authentication controls, encryption, firewalls, and regular security assessments.

3. **Obtain Consent:** Obtain proper consent from clients before collecting, using, or sharing their personal information. Consent should be informed, freely given, and specific to the purposes outlined in the privacy policy.

4. **Provide Notice and Opt-Out Options:** Provide clients with clear notices about their rights and choices regarding the use of their personal information. Allow them to opt out of certain data sharing practices, where applicable.

5. **Train Employees:** Provide training to employees on privacy and data protection practices, emphasizing the importance of confidentiality and compliance with regulations. Employees should understand their responsibilities and how to handle personal information appropriately.

6. **Conduct Privacy Impact Assessments**: Assess the privacy risks associated with new projects, systems, or processes that involve the collection or processing of personal information. Identify and address any privacy concerns before implementation.

7. **Maintain Data Breach Response Plan:** Develop and maintain a comprehensive data breach response plan to address any security incidents involving personal information. This includes timely notification to affected individuals and appropriate authorities, as required by law. This plan should also have a crisis communications component so your firm can mitigate a public relations meltdown.

8. **Regularly Review and Update Practices:** Continuously monitor changes in privacy and data protection laws and adjust practices accordingly. Regularly review and update privacy policies, data handling procedures, and security measures to align with evolving regulatory requirement,

Adhering to legal and compliance requirements is complicated and multi-faceted. It is ultra-important for financial services firms to work with subject matter experts to ensure full compliance with privacy and data protection regulations, as the regulatory landscape is subject to change and can vary based on specific circumstances and jurisdictions.

Conducting regular compliance audits and risk assessments
The frequency of compliance audits and risk assessments can vary depending on factors such as the size of the firm, the nature of its operations, the complexity of regulatory requirements, and the level of risk exposure.

However, it is generally recommended that financial services firms conduct compliance audits and risk assessments on a regular basis to ensure ongoing adherence to regulatory requirements and to identify and mitigate potential risks.

Compliance Audits:
Financial services firms should conduct comprehensive compliance audits **at least annually.** These audits evaluate the firm's adherence to regulatory requirements, internal policies, and procedures. They help identify any gaps or deficiencies in compliance and provide an opportunity to rectify issues before they escalate.

Risk Assessments:
Risk assessments should be conducted periodically, typically **at least annually or more frequently** if there are significant changes in the firm's operations or the regulatory landscape. Risk assessments identify and evaluate potential risks, both internal and external, that could impact the firm's operations and compliance. They help prioritize risk mitigation efforts and inform the development of effective risk management strategies.

Ongoing Monitoring:
In addition to regular audits and risk assessments, financial services firms should establish ongoing monitoring processes to track compliance with regulations and internal policies on a continuous basis. This can include reviewing key metrics, conducting internal reviews, and leveraging technology-based tools to detect and address compliance issues in real-time.

Trigger Events:
Certain events can trigger the need for an **ad hoc compliance audit** or risk assessment. Examples of trigger events include significant regulatory changes, mergers or acquisitions, major operational or technology upgrades, a data breach, or regulatory enforcement actions within the industry. In such cases, financial services firms should conduct audits or risk assessments as appropriate to ensure compliance and manage potential risks.

Clearly, it is important for financial services firms to tailor the frequency of compliance audits and risk assessments to their specific circumstances and the evolving regulatory environment. Frequent monitoring and updates are essential to keep pace with changing regulations, industry best practices, and emerging risks. Additionally, firms should always lean on legal and compliance professionals to determine the appropriate frequency of audits and risk assessments based on their business needs.

Chapter 11: Measuring Marketing Effectiveness and ROI

Some bean counters think of marketing as an optional part of business. Of course, all marketers balk at such blasphemy! The best way to prove the worth of marketing initiatives is with numbers, specifically numbers that measure the return on investment (ROI).

Simply put, ROI numbers show the purse-holders whether the dollars brought to the firm through marketing efforts were greater than or equal to the cost to get them there. For marketers, ROI tells a bigger story: it helps us weigh our own effectiveness, decide if our efforts truly got the results we projected, and just how much we're impacting the firm's bottom line—either positively or negatively.

By tracking and analyzing marketing performance, firms can make data-driven decisions, optimize their strategies, and allocate resources effectively. Here are a few key reasons why measuring marketing effectiveness and ROI is important:

Accountability and Performance Evaluation: Measuring marketing effectiveness allows firms to hold their marketing initiatives accountable. It helps assess whether the marketing activities are meeting their objectives, reaching the target audience, and generating desired outcomes. By evaluating performance, firms can identify how best to allocate resources efficiently.

Resource Allocation and Budget Optimization: Measuring ROI enables financial services firms to determine which marketing channels, campaigns, and tactics are hitting the mark. This information helps in making informed decisions about where to cut or how best to spend. By focusing resources on the most effective strategies, firms can maximize their return on investment and avoid wasting resources on activities that flop.

Identifying Customer Acquisition and Retention: Measuring marketing effectiveness provides insights into customer acquisition and retention rates. It helps firms understand what's working to attract new customers and retain existing ones. This information can guide strategic decisions to improve customer targeting, engagement, and loyalty. It can even help with overall business operations as it may identify a deficiency that prompts a line extension, co-branding opportunity, or ever a corporate merger.

Refining Targeting and Messaging: Financial firms can use ROI to assess the impact of their messaging and targeting strategies. By analyzing customer responses and feedback, firms can refine their messaging to better resonate with the audience. This leads to more effective communication and improved engagement.

Continuous Improvement and Adaptation: Measuring marketing effectiveness provides valuable data for continuous improvement and adaptation. By monitoring performance metrics, firms can identify trends, opportunities, and challenges. This information helps in adjusting marketing strategies, experimenting with new approaches, and staying ahead in a competitive landscape.

Alignment with Business Goals: Measuring marketing effectiveness ensures alignment with overall business goals. It helps the team understand how marketing efforts contribute to the bottom line and support broader business objectives. This alignment fosters strategic decision-making and strengthens the overall marketing strategy.

In summary, measuring marketing effectiveness and ROI allows financial services firms to make informed decisions, optimize their marketing strategies, allocate resources effectively, and align marketing efforts with business goals. It helps drive accountability, improve performance, and maximize the impact of marketing initiatives in a competitive industry.

Let's examine 8 KPIs for financial services marketing

Key Performance Indicators (KPIs) are important metrics that help financial services firms measure the performance and effectiveness of their marketing efforts. Here are some KPIs specifically relevant to financial services marketing:

1. Conversion Rate: The conversion rate measures the percentage of website visitors or leads that take a desired action, such as filling out a form, subscribing to a newsletter, or becoming a customer. In other words, this is the number of people who do what you want. This KPI indicates how effective the marketing efforts are in driving desired outcomes and capturing potential customers.

2. Cost per Lead (CPL): The cost per lead measures the amount of money spent on marketing campaigns or initiatives to acquire a single lead. It helps evaluate the efficiency of marketing investments and allows for cost optimization. Lower CPL indicates more cost-effective marketing efforts.

3. Customer Acquisition Cost (CAC): The customer acquisition cost calculates the average cost to acquire a new customer. It takes into account all marketing and sales expenses involved in acquiring customers. Monitoring CAC helps financial services firms assess the effectiveness of their customer acquisition strategies and evaluate the return on investment.

4. Return on Investment (ROI): ROI measures the profitability and financial impact of marketing initiatives. It compares the revenue generated or the value gained from marketing efforts with the costs incurred. Positive ROI indicates that the marketing activities are generating a net positive return for the firm.

5. Website Traffic and Engagement: Tracking website traffic metrics such as total visits, unique visitors, and page views helps assess the effectiveness of online marketing efforts. Additionally, monitoring engagement metrics like average time spent on the site, bounce rate, and click-through rates provides insights into the user experience and the effectiveness of website content.

6. Customer Lifetime Value (CLTV): Customer Lifetime Value measures the total value a customer brings to the business over their entire relationship with the firm. It helps financial services firms understand the long-term profitability of their customer base and evaluate the effectiveness of customer retention strategies.

7. Social Media Engagement: Monitoring social media engagement metrics such as likes, shares, comments, and followers helps evaluate the effectiveness of social media marketing efforts. It indicates the level of audience engagement, brand awareness, and customer interaction on social platforms.

8. Email Marketing Metrics: For financial services firms that use email marketing, metrics like open rates, click-through rates, conversion rates, and unsubscribe rates are important indicators of email campaign effectiveness and audience engagement.

These are just a few examples of key performance indicators for financial services marketing. It's essential for each firm to identify and track the KPIs that align with their specific marketing goals, objectives, and business model. Regularly monitoring and analyzing these metrics allows firms to make data-driven decisions, optimize their marketing strategies, and drive better results.

Tracking and analyzing marketing metrics and data

Tracking and analyzing marketing metrics and data is essential for financial services firms to measure the effectiveness of their marketing efforts and make data-driven decisions. Here are some common ways to track and analyze marketing metrics and data:

Marketing Analytics Platforms: Utilize marketing analytics platforms like Google Analytics, Adobe Analytics, or HubSpot to track website traffic, user behavior, conversion rates, and other relevant metrics. These platforms provide detailed insights and reports to help analyze marketing performance.

CRM Systems: Implement a customer relationship management (CRM) system that allows tracking and analyzing customer interactions, sales data, and marketing campaigns. Effective, up-to-date CRM systems can help consolidate customer data and provide insights into marketing effectiveness and customer engagement.

Social Media Analytics: Use social media analytics tools provided by social platforms (such as Facebook Insights, X (formerly Twitter) Analytics, or LinkedIn Analytics) to track engagement metrics, reach, impressions, and audience demographics. These tools help measure the impact of social media marketing efforts.

Email Marketing Platforms: If using email marketing, leverage platforms like Mailchimp, Constant Contact, or Campaign Monitor, which offer analytics and reporting features. These platforms provide data on email open rates, click-through rates, and other email campaign performance metrics.

Custom Tracking and Tagging: Implement custom tracking and tagging mechanisms using UTM parameters (a string of letters added to the end of a URL) or tracking pixels to monitor the performance of specific campaigns, channels, or marketing initiatives. This allows for more granular tracking and analysis of marketing efforts.

Data Visualization Tools: Employ data visualization tools such as Tableau, Power BI, or Google Data Studio to create visual representations of marketing data. These tools enable easy interpretation and analysis of complex marketing metrics through interactive dashboards and reports. Sometimes a picture is worth a thousand words.

A/B Testing: Conduct A/B testing or split testing to compare the performance of different marketing strategies or variations of marketing assets. A/B testing provides data-driven insights into what resonates best with the target audience and helps optimize marketing efforts.

Surveys and Feedback: Gather customer feedback and conduct surveys to gain insights into customer satisfaction, preferences, and perceptions. This qualitative data complements quantitative metrics and helps understand the effectiveness of marketing campaigns from the customer's perspective.

Regular Reporting and Analysis: Establish a regular reporting schedule to review and analyze marketing metrics and data. This could be weekly, monthly, or quarterly reports that highlight key performance indicators, trends, and areas for improvement.

By leveraging these tracking and analysis methods, financial services firms can gain valuable insights into their marketing performance, identify areas for optimization, and make data-driven decisions to drive better results. It's important to regularly review and analyze the data to continuously refine marketing strategies and improve marketing effectiveness.

Assessing the ROI of marketing initiatives

In order to assess whether your marketing activities have been fruitful, you need to begin with a projection or a goal in mind. Failing to compare your actual results to your expected results keeps you chasing your tail, never knowing if the dollars spent have been spent well. Here are some best practices to see if what you're doing is getting the results you want and need to defend your activities and hopefully grow your budget to keep pushing forward.

1. Set Clear Objectives:
   Clearly define the objectives and goals of your marketing initiatives. Whether it's increasing brand awareness, generating leads, or driving conversions, having well-defined objectives helps align ROI assessment with specific outcomes.

2. Establish Key Performance Indicators (KPIs):
   Identify the key metrics and KPIs that align with your marketing goals and objectives. These could include metrics like conversion rate, customer acquisition cost (CAC), customer lifetime value (CLTV), revenue generated, or other relevant metrics specific to your marketing objectives. Your KPIs are and should be unique to your firm's needs.

3. Track and Attribute Marketing Expenses:
   Accurately track all marketing expenses associated with your initiatives, including campaign costs, advertising spend, staff time, technology and software costs, and any other relevant expenses. This ensures that you have a comprehensive view of your marketing investment.

4. Implement Proper Tracking Mechanisms:
   Utilize tracking mechanisms like unique URLs, UTM parameters, tracking pixels, or dedicated phone numbers to attribute conversions or sales to specific marketing campaigns or channels. This allows for more accurate measurement of the impact of your marketing efforts.

5. Calculate ROI:
   Calculate the ROI by comparing the revenue or value generated from your marketing initiatives with the total costs incurred.

   The formula for ROI is: (Net Profit / Marketing Investment) x 100.

   Net Profit is the revenue generated minus the total costs. This calculation provides a percentage that represents the return on your marketing investment.

6. Consider Time and Attribution Windows: Take into account the time it takes for marketing initiatives to yield results and consider attribution windows. Some marketing efforts may have longer-term impacts, so it's important to evaluate ROI over an appropriate time frame and attribute conversions appropriately.

7. Compare Against Benchmarks:

    Benchmark your ROI against industry averages or past performance to gain a better
    understanding of how your marketing efforts are performing relative to others in the
    industry. This helps provide context and identify areas for improvement.

8. Regularly Analyze and Optimize:
    Continuously analyze the ROI of your marketing initiatives and identify areas for
    optimization. Use the insights gained from ROI assessment to refine your marketing
    strategies, allocate resources effectively, and invest in initiatives that provide the
    highest return.

9. Use Marketing Analytics Tools:
    Leverage marketing analytics platforms or tools to automate data collection, analysis,
    and reporting. These tools provide real-time insights and visualizations that facilitate
    ROI assessment and make it easier to track and optimize marketing efforts.

By following these best practices, financial services firms can effectively assess the ROI of their
marketing initiatives and make informed decisions to optimize their marketing strategies,
allocate resources efficiently, and achieve better results.

*Remember, ROI assessment should be an ongoing process to ensure continuous improvement
and maximize the return on your marketing investment. The number crunching never ends.

Making data-driven decisions for continuous improvement
Data is your friend. Pinpointing real data points and being able to produce real numbers that
reflect the impact your activities have on the firm's bottom line keeps you prepared to answer
questions from anyone who asks. When budgets are lean, data will help you whittle down
marketing activities to those that have proven to generate the best results.

Financial services firms can make data-driven decisions for continuous improvement by
following these key steps:

1. Define Clear Objectives: Start by clearly defining the objectives you want to achieve.
    Whether it's increasing customer acquisition, improving customer retention, optimizing
    marketing campaigns, or enhancing operational efficiency, having specific goals helps
    guide your data analysis efforts.

2. Identify Relevant Data: Determine the types of data that are relevant to your
    objectives. This may include customer data, sales data, marketing metrics, website

analytics, financial performance data, and more. Identify the key data sources that will provide insights into your objectives.

3. Collect and Consolidate Data: Ensure you have processes in place to collect and consolidate the relevant data. This may involve integrating data from multiple sources, such as CRM systems, marketing analytics platforms, financial systems, and other data repositories. Data quality and integrity are crucial, so implement measures to ensure accuracy and completeness.

4. Analyze and Interpret Data: Use data analysis techniques to uncover meaningful insights. This may involve using statistical analysis, data visualization tools, or predictive modeling to identify patterns, trends, and correlations in the data. Look for insights that can inform decision-making and highlight areas for improvement.

5. Apply Data to Decision-Making: Once you have analyzed the data and gained insights, use this information to guide your decision-making processes. Evaluate the potential impact of different options based on the data-driven insights. This could include optimizing marketing strategies, refining product offerings, adjusting pricing, or improving operational processes.

6. Monitor and Measure Results: Implement mechanisms to monitor the outcomes of your decisions. Continuously measure the impact of the changes you have made based on the data-driven decisions. This allows you to assess the effectiveness of your decisions and make further adjustments as needed.

7. Foster a Data-Driven Culture: Promote a culture of data-driven decision-making within your organization. Encourage stakeholders to rely on data and insights rather than intuition or anecdotal evidence. Provide training and resources to enhance data literacy among employees and empower them to use data in their decision-making processes.

8. Continuously Improve: Embrace a mindset of continuous improvement based on the insights gained from data analysis. Regularly review and assess your strategies, processes, and outcomes. Identify areas for further optimization and use data to inform your efforts to drive ongoing improvement.

9. Invest in Technology and Expertise: Ensure that you have the necessary technology infrastructure and expertise to collect, analyze, and interpret data effectively. This may involve investing in data analytics tools, hiring data analysts or data scientists, or partnering with external experts who can provide valuable insights and recommendations.

By making data-driven decisions and continuously leveraging data for improvement, financial services firms can enhance their operations, customer experiences, and overall business performance. Data-driven decision-making helps optimize strategies, mitigate risks, and drive growth in a rapidly evolving industry.

Chapter 12: THE BIG WRAP UP

So, what did we learn in this book?

I'm including this TL/DR version of all the previous pages (though, I strongly suggest you make your way through those in small doses because they have some valuable insights).

Here are the 8 essential best practices for financial services marketing in the USA.

1. Embrace Digital Transformation: Recognize the importance of digital channels and technologies in reaching and engaging with your target audience. Adapt your marketing strategies to leverage the power of websites, social media, email marketing, mobile apps, and other digital platforms.

2. Prioritize Personalization: Tailor your marketing efforts to meet the specific needs and preferences of your target audience. Leverage customer data and segmentation to deliver personalized experiences, offers, and communications.

3. Focus on Content Marketing: Create valuable and relevant content that educates, informs, and engages your audience. Develop thought leadership through whitepapers, articles, blog posts, and other content formats that position your firm as an industry expert and provide valuable insights to clients and prospects.

4. Build a Strong Online Presence: Establish a robust online presence through an engaging website, active social media presence, and effective SEO strategies. Leverage digital marketing channels to increase brand visibility, generate leads, and drive conversions.

5. Foster Client Relationships: Implement relationship marketing strategies to establish and nurture client relationships. Regularly communicate with clients, provide personalized experiences, and offer exceptional customer service to build trust and loyalty.

6. Compliance and Ethical Practices: Stay abreast of regulatory rules and guidelines specific to the financial services industry. Adhere to ethical standards in marketing practices, safeguard customer data, and maintain transparency to build trust with clients.

7. Utilize Data and Analytics: Leverage customer data and marketing analytics to make data-driven decisions. Track and analyze KPIs to measure marketing effectiveness and ROI. Use insights to optimize marketing strategies and improve decision-making.

8. Adapt to Changing Trends: Continuously monitor and adapt to the evolving marketing landscape. Embrace innovative strategies and technologies to stay ahead in the

industry. Keep a pulse on emerging trends, consumer behaviors, and technological advancements to remain competitive.

By following these best practices, financial services firms can effectively navigate the dynamic marketing landscape. Embrace innovation, stay customer-centric, and leverage data to drive marketing success, build strong client relationships, and ultimately achieve business growth and success.

In other words, do all this and you'll **get them to buy.**

KEY TERMS

Brand Awareness- The level of familiarity and recognition that the target audience has with a financial services firm's brand name, logo, or offerings.

Call-to-Action (CTA)- A prompt or instruction that encourages the target audience to take a specific action, such as "Request a Quote" or "Sign Up Today."

Compliance- The adherence to regulatory rules, laws, and guidelines governing financial services marketing practices to ensure ethical and legal conduct.

Content Marketing- The creation and distribution of valuable, relevant, and informative content to attract and engage the target audience, with the ultimate goal of driving profitable customer action.

Conversion Rate- The percentage of leads or prospects that become paying customers or take a desired action, such as opening an account or making a purchase.

Customer Lifetime Value (CLV)- The predicted value of a customer to a financial services firm over the course of their relationship, including revenue from repeat purchases or engagements.

Customer Relationship Management (CRM)- A system or software used to manage and analyze customer interactions, information, and relationships, helping to improve customer retention and satisfaction.

Lead Generation- The process of attracting and capturing potential customers' interest in a financial product or service, often through various marketing activities.

Pay-Per-Click (PPC) Advertising- A digital advertising model where advertisers pay a fee each time their ad is clicked, often used in search engine advertising or display advertising.

Positioning- The way a financial services firm presents itself and its offerings in the market, creating a distinct and favorable perception in the minds of the target audience.

Return on Investment (ROI)- The measurement of the profitability or effectiveness of marketing campaigns or activities, comparing the investment made to the resulting financial returns.

Search Engine Optimization (SEO)- The practice of optimizing a financial services firm's website and content to rank higher in search engine results, increasing visibility and organic traffic.

Segmentation- The process of dividing the target audience into distinct groups based on characteristics such as demographics, behaviors, or needs. This allows for more personalized marketing strategies.

Target Audience- The specific group of individuals or businesses that a financial services firm aims to reach and serve with its marketing efforts.

Value Proposition- The unique benefits and value that a financial services firm offers to its target audience, differentiating it from competitors.

Please note that the definitions provided are concise explanations of each term. For a more comprehensive understanding, it is advisable to refer to the detailed definitions and context within the financial services marketing field.

About the author:

AC Hoffmann has worked in marketing since 1996, engaged on both the agency side and within various *Fortune* 500 corporations, including life insurance companies, asset management firms, and financial consultancies. This work is a collection of knowledge gained over several decades of marketing such services b2b and b2c.

www.ingramcontent.com/pod-product-compliance
Lightning Source LLC
Chambersburg PA
CBHW080938260726
48661CB00010B/3977